In Search of the Fourth Freedom

In
Search
of the
Fourth
Freedom

By

HOWARD S. BREMBECK

Second Edition

University of Notre Dame Press

Notre Dame, Indiana

Second Edition 2000
Published by University of Notre Dame Press
Notre Dame, Indiana 46556
www.undpress.nd.edu

Manufactured in the United States of America

Library of Congress Cataloging-in-Publication Data
Brembeck, Howard S.
    In search of the fourth freedom / by Howard S. Brembeck.
    p.   cm.
Includes index.
    ISBN 0-268-03151-7 (cloth : alk. paper) —
    ISBN 0-268-03152-5 (paper : alk. paper)
    1. Nuclear disarmament.   2. Security, International.
3. International trade.   I. Title.
JZ5665.B74   2000
327.1′747—dc21   00-025641

The paper used in this publication meets the minimum requirements
of the American National Standard for Information Sciences—Permanence of
Paper for Printed Library Materials, ANSI Z39.48—1984

Contents

Contents

Foreword

Where there is no vision, reads the scripture, the people perish. In much of public life today leaders sorely lack vision. Cynicism tends to prevail over hope, and few have the imagination to look beyond today toward creating a better tomorrow. Lack of vision is not a problem for Howard Brembeck, the founder and chairman of the Fourth Freedom Forum. *In Search of the Fourth Freedom* is a visionary book that examines the means of creating a more civilized world. It is a far-sighted but practical plan for using the power of trade to help free the world from the fear of weapons of mass destruction and the age old tyranny of war, terrorism and genocide. It is a vision which our chaotic world desperately needs.

Howard Brembeck is an extraordinary figure, a genuine Horatio Alger American success story. Born in a small farming community in northern Indiana, he became a self-made millionaire in classic entrepreneurial fashion. He designed and manufactured grain storage and poultry feeding equipment that revolutionized the farming industry and dramatically improved agricultural productivity worldwide. While traveling the globe to promote his products, now sold in more than 100 countries, he witnessed firsthand the power of trade to bring people together and raise living standards. He also saw the folly and destructiveness of war and the madness of accumulating massive stockpiles of nuclear weapons. From these insights and experiences arose the conviction that there must be a better way. The result was the Civilized Defense Plan, a program for outlawing weapons of mass destruction and using the power of trade to enforce civilized standards of behavior.

In Search of the Fourth Freedom lights the way to a brighter future by applying the hard lessons of history. The twentieth century experienced two world wars and countless conflicts. We have seen the appalling economic devastation wrought by war. Since 1945 we have lived under the shadow of nuclear apocalypse. But we have also learned that liberty must be protected against the tyrants who inevitably attempt to trample it. We know that nations must have a system of effective defense to preserve their security.

The dilemma is how to defend freedom without falling prey to military madness. The solution is close at hand, in the world of business and commerce. History teaches that trade and economic development play a dominant role in shaping the course of human events. Civilizations rise or fall according to their productive capacity and economic vitality. The greatest force in the world is not military might but commerce, the insatiable drive of people everywhere to improve their lives by trading. This power can be harnessed to help tame aggression and overcome the scourge of war. Two hundred years ago the great German philosopher Immanuel Kant wrote: "It is the spirit of commerce which cannot coexist with war, and which sooner or later takes hold of every nation." The nineteenth century British philosopher John Stuart Mill argued similarly that "the great extent and rapid increase of international trade [is] the principal guarantee of the peace of the world."

Howard Brembeck gained his insights into the power of trade not from philosophy books but from a lifetime of practical experience. He saw how commerce increases interaction and understanding, creating a mutual interdependence that is the very antithesis of armed conflict. How the power of withholding, by denying what the other party wants, can motivate a change in the terms of what is offered in response. From these observations, Brembeck distilled the simple but elegant propositions that form the foundation of his Civilized Defense Plan. Humankind can free itself from the fear of annihilation by using the power of trade to enforce an international ban on aggression and weapons of mass destruction. Through a more forceful and creative use of economic sanctions and incentives, it may be possible to create a fundamentally different way of preserving security.

The Fourth Freedom Forum was founded to develop the ideas in the Civilized Defense Plan. It draws its inspiration from Franklin Delano

Roosevelt's famous 1941 speech on the Four Freedoms, the fourth of which is Freedom from Fear, which Roosevelt defined as "a worldwide reduction in armaments, to such a point and in such thorough fashion that no nation will be in a position to commit an act of physical aggression against any neighbor, anywhere in the world." In recent years the Forum has sponsored conferences, published books and reports, and consulted with the UN Security Council, the UN Department of Humanitarian Affairs, the Council on Foreign Relations, the Carter Center, and the Carnegie Commission on Preventing Deadly Conflict. The result has been a constant refinement of the Civilized Defense Plan.

When the Forum was created in the 1980s at the height of the cold war, the idea of banning weapons of mass destruction seemed utopian. So did the concept of relying on the power of trade through economic sanctions and incentives. Since the late 1980s, however, these ideas have steadily gained acceptance and support. Nuclear weapons are being sharply reduced. The comprehensive test ban has been signed. A treaty banning chemical weapons is now in place. The idea of eliminating nuclear weapons entirely, once dismissed as impossible, is now advocated by former high-ranking military officers. Since 1990 multilateral economic sanctions have been imposed with increasing frequency. UN officials are giving greater attention to the concept of "smart sanctions," the targeting of pressures against the leaders responsible for wrongdoing rather than vulnerable populations.

A greater reliance on economic power has many advantages over the traditional resort to military violence. Where war destroys, economic power has the ability to create. When trade benefits and economic assistance are offered as incentives, the benefits accrue not only to recipients but to senders as well. The use of incentives is a classic win-win strategy that can bring the fruits of cooperation to both parties. Reducing our reliance on weapons can free nations from the burden of unnecessary and wasteful military spending. The weight of cold war military spending helped to bring down the Soviet Union. The U.S. military budget remains at near cold war levels ($289 billion in 2000) and is a continuing drain on the productivity of the American economy, to say nothing of the enormous tax burden it imposes. Adopting the principles of the Civilized Defense Plan would allow the United States and other nations to reduce the burden of military expenditure and devote additional resources to improving people's lives. The result would be greater prosperity and a better life for all.

Brembeck's vision is idealistic, yes, but it is not utopian. It does not mean that wars or aggression will magically disappear. It is not based on a naive faith in human goodness. It recognizes that nations must remain vigilant against the evils of totalitarianism, and that collective defense, even with military means, sometimes may be necessary. But it places the primary responsibility for assuring security on economic power rather than weapons, and it insists that nations get serious about eliminating the continuing threat of nuclear destruction. It asks only that we recognize the trends that are already underway, toward increased use of economic power and decreased emphasis on nuclear weaponry, and that we pursue these developments to their logical conclusion.

Brembeck's ideas deserve wide consideration. For too long nations have relied on ever bigger and more powerful weapons to protect themselves. Since the beginning of human history war and the pursuit of military power have been abiding preoccupations. Great academies and institutions have been created to study and advance the science of war. By contrast, the use of economic power is in its infancy, with little attention or research devoted to its improvement. It is long past time to remedy this imbalance and devote greater resources and energy to the urgent task of finding a better and more secure way of preserving peace. *In Search of the Fourth Freedom* points the way forward.

David Cortright
President
Fourth Freedom Forum

Acknowledgments

This book is the work of many people who have shared their insights and experience and helped me articulate the search for the Fourth Freedom. I am especially grateful for the substantial contributions of James Carroll and David Cortright. Carroll helped translate my thoughts into words and Cortright provided expert analysis on economic sanctions and incentives as well as international policy developments.

The writing of this book received important assistance from the staff of the Fourth Freedom Forum, especially Alistair Millar, Jennifer Glick, and Ann Pedler. I am indebted to the Fourth Freedom Forum staff for their constant encouragement and support. Special thanks are also due the directors of the Fourth Freedom Forum who read the manuscript and in many cases provided substantive comment: Charles W. Ainlay, General George Lee Butler (Air Force Ret.), J. Lawrence Burkholder, John C. Frieden, Reverend Andrew L. Hardie, Miriam J. Redsecker, William P. Johnson, George A. Lopez, Frank K. Martin, and LeRoy Troyer.

In the course of thinking about and writing this book I have had the privilege of meeting many policy experts and former government and military officials. Among those who have commented on the manuscript or shared their insights with me are President Jimmy Carter, Reverend Theodore M. Hesburgh, C.S.C., Admiral Stansfield Turner (Navy Ret.), Admiral Eugene Carroll (Navy Ret.), Richard Haass, Jonathan Schell, Benjamin Ferencz, Harry Barnes, and David Krieger.

My greatest debt of gratitude is owed to my wife of sixty-six years, Myra Brembeck, who has been my constant source of encouragement and inspiration.

Introduction

The guns of World War II had long been silent. The terror of the bombs and the suffering of the innocent were fading into a nightmare memory. But the words of two men echoed in my mind.

One was Franklin D. Roosevelt. The other was Albert Einstein.

In a 1941 address to Congress, President Roosevelt had outlined his vision of the Four Freedoms: Freedom of Speech, Freedom of Religion, Freedom from Want and Freedom from Fear. He said:

> The fourth is freedom from fear, which translated into world terms, means a worldwide reduction in armaments, to such a point and in such a thorough fashion that no nation will be in a position to commit an act of aggression against any neighbor, anywhere in the world.

His words inspired millions during the war and they continued to provide inspiration as the war's violence drifted into the chilling reality of the Cold War. But the more I looked at the world around me, the more I concluded that he was describing an unrealistic dream, an unattainable goal.

Still, there was magic in the dream, worthiness in the goal. I refused to let go of the dream or to take my eyes off the goal. Instead, I repeatedly called to mind the admonition of Einstein:

> The unleashed power of the atom has changed everything save our modes of thinking, and thus we drift toward unparalleled catastrophe. We shall require a substantially new manner of thinking if mankind is to survive.

With new modes of thinking, perhaps the world would achieve Freedom from Fear. Perhaps the very real threat of world-destroying nuclear war could be averted. Then on a September day in 1979, my worries about a nuclear holocaust and my visualization of the Fourth Freedom dream began to transform themselves into concepts more concrete.

I was traveling in England and thinking about a strategy to solve a business problem when it occurred to me that the concepts I was considering might be applied to the confrontation between the United States and the Soviet Union. These concepts might move the world back from the nuclear abyss. I didn't know it at the time, but the search for the Fourth Freedom had begun.

Like every entrepreneur, I had found that business pressures often required me to do some creative thinking. I also had done my best to acquire the habit of letting my imagination run wild from time to time. As I puzzled over the nuclear dilemma, I came to see the power of trade as a possible solution. Perhaps the giving (incentives) and the withholding (sanctions) of economic benefit could help to tame the scourge of war and eliminate the threat of nuclear annihilation. I had doubts at first. Perhaps my thoughts on international relationships were impractical. If they were exposed to the light of reality, perhaps they would disappear in a few days. But they didn't. Instead, they commanded my attention with such persistence that I felt compelled to devote more and more time and energy to my search.

In 1982, I established the Fourth Freedom Forum as a focal point for the discussion of international security issues, especially those involving the innovative utilization of economic power. Today, the Forum is a viable organization that has gained international recognition as an objective, reliable source of information on the effectiveness of incentives and sanctions.

Through the Forum, I was able to draw on the insights and experience of knowledgeable people in the military, the foreign relations community, academia and the United Nations. Our discussions helped refine my thoughts and enabled me to write a book, *The Civilized Defense Plan: Security of Nations Through the Power of Trade*, published in 1989. At the time, the book seemed visionary, more dream than operational plan.

When it was written, no one had predicted that the Berlin Wall soon would fall and the Soviet Union would disintegrate. Few could have imagined that the Cold War would soon be over and the number of nuclear weapons would be radically reduced.

A decade ago, economic sanctions were disdained by most foreign affairs experts. So were incentives, the reverse side of the sanctions coin. The success attributed to economic power in the United Nations' effort to dampen hostilities in the former Yugoslavia could not have been foreseen. Neither could the achievement of sanctions in isolating Saddam Hussein for a prolonged period and inhibiting, if not ending, his aggressive behavior.

What most of us believed about international relationships a decade or so ago has undergone a significant transformation. The necessity of universally observed international law is acknowledged by an increasing number of influential people in America and around the world. So is the importance of effective, nonviolent law enforcement. Given these developments and the trends they signify, I now see that Roosevelt's dream was not as unrealistic as I originally believed. New modes of thinking no longer are relegated to the backbenches of the parliament of ideas. I now understand that dreams are essential to creative thinking and the Fourth Freedom is achievable.

Yet, the reign of fear is far from over. As we have learned from events in Iraq, even a small, impoverished nation has the potential to produce horrifying weapons. India and Pakistan have conducted nuclear weapons tests that intensify regional hostilities and underscore the continuing dangers of proliferation. A struggling, unstable Russian Federation retains possession of thousands of weapons of mass destruction. Terrorists, gangsters and fanatics have learned that the secrets of producing these weapons are no longer hidden. Weapons-grade nuclear materials and even the weapons themselves could easily fall into the hands of black marketeers and blackmailers.

As the world's only economic and military superpower, the United States has no reason to be afraid of any nation on earth. It can concentrate on seeking a world free of aggression, state-sponsored terrorism and the unspeakable evil of genocide. America's unchallenged world leadership has given it a special responsibility to build a just and effective system of international security. The only questions that need to be answered have to do with our wisdom and our resolve. Are we wise enough to build a world ruled by the force of law, not the law of force?

In searching for a new manner of thinking about power, we must consider America's strength in the context of history. Then we will understand that no nation—not even one as strong as present day America—can forever force its will on the rest of the world. If we give the matter sufficient thought, we realize that the only way America can continue its leadership is through creation of a system of effective global law. By accepting our role in helping to create a lawful world, we will be building a society in which all nations and all people will have the law as their advocate whenever they suffer injustice at the hands of law violators.

This is an attainable goal and the proof can be found in post–World War II Europe. As a businessman, I found myself dealing with people in Germany and Italy, nations that had been our enemies only a few years before. I was witnessing a flow of trade between Germany, France, Great Britain and other countries that had been fighting with each other for decades. I found it ironic that my company was doing business in Japan, our World War II opponent, but not in the Soviet Union, our World War II ally. I also noticed that the exchange of goods seemed to be healing ancient wounds and erasing hatreds that extended back for hundreds of years.

My observations forced me to ask myself some difficult questions. What is it that provokes nations to war against each other? What are the root causes of the mass insanity that causes people to commit indescribable atrocities? Why do men and women who know they are supposed to love their neighbors adopt hatred as a guiding principle? And when the fighting stops, what thought processes enable people who once were enemies to come together with courtesy, respect and, after a time, with understanding bordering on genuine affection?

Such questions are central to the search for the Fourth Freedom and they deserve thoughtful consideration. For Americans, the starting point is a conscious effort to shake off ignorance, conquer the blinding arrogance that is an understandable consequence of national success, overcome our worries about the unknown and shed the light of truth into the dark corners of our thinking. Then we need to adopt a civilized plan of action.

I believe the plan that I outlined in my earlier book and which I further develop in this one can play a significant role in pushing back the boundaries of fear. It would put the nations of the world under the rule of law and provide an effective, fair and humane system of enforcement.

I realized from the start that my ideas might be rejected out of hand by the foreign policy establishment. Although I did not hesitate to seek the advice of experts, I refused to accept the cynicism and insularity of conventional wisdom. My years in business taught me the importance of change, innovation and risk. Applying these ideas to international security seemed radical at first. But a balanced assessment of recent events indicates that mainstream thinking is changing, perhaps even moving toward a civilized defense. More people have come to understand that new modes of thinking are essential to human survival.

New thinking necessarily involves an element of risk. Indeed, risk is built into the human experience. If we want to accomplish anything of importance, risk cannot be avoided. There was risk in the Marshall Plan when we gave of ourselves to help a defeated foe and enabled democracy to rise from the ashes of dictatorship. There will be risk when, at long last, we join other nations in outlawing nuclear and all other weapons of mass murder and in creating an institutionalized system for the international enforcement of the rule of law. But the payoff will be tremendous. I can see now that it could literally lift us to a higher level of living.

I invite you to join me in a search for the Fourth Freedom.

CHAPTER ONE

A New Road
to an Old Dream

The empires of the future are the empires of the mind.

—Winston Churchill

As an eyewitness to more than eight decades of the twentieth century, I am convinced we are living in one of our history's most remarkable periods. It is an age of limitless opportunity. The power of the individual has been unshackled. Men and women in every country, on every continent, have more reason than ever to be confident of themselves and their future. They have the tools to make dreams come true.

The development of the silicon chip and all of its progeny has accelerated the explosive growth of a personal communications network of astonishing power and pervasiveness. We have access to equipment that was undreamed of through much of my life—mobile telephones, computers, facsimile machines and a variety of other transmitting and receiving devices that utilize fiber optic cables, microprocessors, satellites and other electronic gear. Through this network, everyday individuals now have instantaneous access to civilization's storehouse of information and experience. They can tap into the thoughts and concerns of people in every corner of the world. They can act globally to reach goals that have eluded their leaders for centuries. Ordinary people now have the ability to eradicate the culture of war and create an environment that will enable humanity to live up to its potential.

Never before has the individual possessed so much power to profoundly influence the present and the future. Today's expanding empowerment of the individual marks a turning point in the development of civilization. We have reached a moment in which we can begin to visualize a future dominated by hope. We have begun to cross the threshold into an age controlled by realistic thinking about the nature of international relationships. I strongly believe we are moving closer to a world in which aggression can be outlawed and security will be made genuine.

War's Roll Call of Death and Destruction

During my lifetime, war has taken as many as 100 million lives. More than half of the victims were civilians, most of them entirely innocent of wrongdoing. Countless others were wounded or impoverished. Resources were squandered. Lives were disrupted. Intellectual energy was focused on developing more efficient ways to kill others, not on creating the tools and techniques that sustain life or elevate it to a higher level of existence.

In the roll call of death, the United States does not rank among the nations most seriously affected by the wars of the twentieth century. The number of American servicemen who lost their lives in combat in World Wars I and II is in excess of 400,000, a number that seems small compared to the millions who died in Russia, Germany, France and other nations. Yet, nearly every American family was touched in some way by the loss of a loved one and reminders of their sacrifice stand in town squares and cemeteries in communities, large and small, from Maine to California.

Those who died gave, as Abraham Lincoln put it, the "last full measure of devotion," to their country and its cause. They and their comrades in arms contributed to the allied victory of 1918 and, a quarter century later, they played a leading role in bringing both Germany and Japan to their knees. In Europe, Asia and other corners of the world, the men and women of our armed forces repeatedly demonstrated America's commitment to justice and democracy. They proved that U.S. leadership is an essential ingredient in any recipe for international security.

Growing Threats to Civilization

Now U.S. leadership is being challenged to meet a threat that may prove to be more difficult and deadly than any of the past. The end of the Cold War has destabilized many international relationships. Huge stockpiles of nuclear, chemical and biological weapons continue to exist and a number of smaller nations have accelerated their efforts to build their own deadly arsenals.

Terrorists equipped with weapons of devastating potency can slaughter millions in a matter of seconds. They can poison the air and the water supply, disrupt the functions of government and destabilize society. Weapons that can easily be smuggled across borders and concealed in strategic locations already are available and we can expect their power and reliability to increase at a rapid pace during the years ahead.

On every populated continent, ethnic minorities, repressed religious groups or the economically disadvantaged are waging violent war against their neighbors, tearing the social fabric and upsetting the status quo. They seek to overturn the existing system and gain dominance over those they see as unjust dominators. In many cases, the armed struggle extends beyond national borders, threatening regional security and testing the world's determination to enforce peaceful behavior.

The frustration felt by civilized society is evident. The world's great powers appear to be powerless when it comes to eliminating ethnic and religious conflict, terrorism and genocide. Bombs explode in London, Paris, New York and Oklahoma City, poison gas is introduced into the Tokyo subway system, commercial airliners are blasted from the sky, hundreds of thousands of individuals are murdered in cold blood for no other reason than their identification with an ethnic group or tribal organization. Hundreds of thousands of others are driven from their homes to die of hunger or exposure. Armies of diplomats and security officers do their best to end the carnage but they appear to be as ineffective against terrorists and genocidal murderers as the Maginot Line was against the blitzkrieg.

Practitioners of terrorism view it as an instrument of retribution for offenses they attribute to the United States and other democratic nations. They see terrorism as a means of offsetting the economic and military advantages of their perceived enemies. They will not hesitate to use it in their effort to destroy all who have earned their hatred. To defeat terrorism, we will need to increase our awareness of the threat, improve the technology of weapons identification and, most important of all, strengthen our resolve.

We've already seen many examples of what our resolve can accomplish. Because of it, Hitler and the Japanese militarists were defeated. Then in the years after World War II, America's resolve kept the Soviet Union from conquering or subverting Western Europe. For more than four decades, the two superpowers were locked in a battle of wills that produced a strange and thoroughly unjustified sense of security in the minds of many.

Mutually Assured Destruction Becomes Obsolete

Then came the 1991 collapse of the Soviet Union, an event as earth-shaking as it was unexpected. Suddenly, the supposed absolutes of Cold War diplomacy were demolished like the Berlin Wall. The bipolar balance of nuclear power that to some offered a tenuous assurance of world peace was replaced by a fragmented and unreliable sharing of nuclear responsibility. The doctrine of mutually assured destruction and its derivatives, long fixtures in the minds of at least some of the world's policymakers, had become as irrelevant as the treaties that once sought to guarantee peace by establishing quotas for the battleships of potential combatants.

The first reaction to the shattering of the Soviet Union was a wave of hope that swept across America and around the world. The superpower long thought to be fully prepared to march against Western Europe or China or anywhere else suddenly was seen as a paper tiger. The great nation with an arsenal of nuclear weapons, many of them targeted on the United States, abruptly revealed itself to be lacking the unity and the economic resources to survive much less implement some grand scheme for world domination.

Like many people in many parts of the world, I was elated. Democratic capitalism had prevailed. Centralized Marxist economics was discredited. The determination of all who stood in opposition to the Soviets and their plans seemed about to be rewarded. The opportunity to achieve lasting peace seemed closer than ever before.

After the Cold War, Frightening Realities

Then people started to understand that the end of the Soviet Union was far from an unmixed blessing. The demise of a superpower created a diplomatic vacuum. The weakening of what had been the Soviet military created new worries about the ultimate control of a terrifying array of missiles dug into the landscape of Russia, cruising in the oceans of the world or carried aloft by fleets of aircraft. Where are they aimed now and, of equal importance, who is aiming them?

And what about the other confessed or closeted members of the nuclear club? How will they react to a world that no longer revolves around the Cold War's dance of death? Will nonmembers be content to continue to face their enemies without weapons of mass destruction or will the threat to territory or sovereignty, real or perceived, inspire even the poorest nations to pay their dues and gain admittance to the world's most exclusive and dangerous fraternity?

Iraq, Iran, Libya, North Korea, Syria and other nations already have committed huge shares of their resources to the pursuit of nuclear, biological and chemical weapons. In nations of the former Soviet Union, nuclear weapons are being dismantled. But this hopeful development is counterbalanced by the realization that it has become more difficult to account for each warhead, especially tactical nuclear warheads, some small enough to fit in a suitcase. In addition, the dismantling of weapons may increase the availability of weapons-grade nuclear materials. As a result, nuclear bombs or their components may be more available than ever to international troublemakers, terrorist groups or even to racketeers and psychopaths.

With the demise of the Soviet Union, the neat symmetry of the Cold War's balance of terror has been replaced by a patchwork assortment of questions and challenges. Peace no longer can be brokered by two superpowers working out of self-interest to keep the lid on disputes that could quickly boil over into full-fledged war. In the post–Cold War era, peace requires multinational understanding, involvement and, above all, goodwill. It demands, to repeat the words of Einstein, ". . . a substantially new manner of thinking."

Change Has Rendered Military Power Obsolete

Yet, I believe an objective analysis of the statements and actions of many of today's political leaders will reveal that their thinking continues to lag well behind the course of events. They are ill-prepared to deal with today's reality. They do not seem to understand the currents of change that have transformed and are continuing to transform the world. In area after area of urgent concern, they seem unable to comprehend that some of their most cherished beliefs about power have been rendered obsolete by time, trade and technology.

Nowhere is this obsolescence more evident than in the world's continued reliance on military force. In the 1960s and 70s, the United States sacrificed thousands of lives and billions of dollars in a vain effort to achieve what it perceived as our national objectives in Vietnam. The Soviet Union, apparently learning nothing from the experience of its superpower rival, followed much the same scenario in Afghanistan. Then Iraq invaded Iran to begin a winnerless, marathon war that produced many casualties but nothing that could be defined as a victory for either side.

The Gulf War: An Exercise in Frustration

In the Persian Gulf war, Iraq used chemical weapons to neutralize the human wave tactics of Iranian volunteers. The use was a clear violation of international law but under the don't-rock-the-boat diplomatic doctrine of the Cold War years, the world's great powers did their best to ignore the transgression. They took no definitive action to punish Iraq for behavior that violated the accepted norms of civilized society. The failure to respond, the refusal by the United States, the Soviet Union and other states to do what is right, undoubtedly emboldened Saddam Hussein. He accelerated his quest for weapons of mass destruction and he continued his aggressive conduct. Before long, he was flexing his military muscle by marching into Kuwait and up to the doorstep of Saudi Arabia.

On a matter of principle—that is, the use by Iraq of illegal weapons—the industrialized nations turned their backs. On a matter of economic interest—that is, control of a substantial share of the world's crude oil supply—the industrialized nations took firm and immediate action. Under the leadership of the United States, they organized a devastating multinational response, a military campaign that succeeded in forcing the Iraqis out of Kuwait.

At the time, it seemed a glorious victory. But joy soon gave way to disappointment. While the stability of the oil-rich region appeared to have been at least temporarily preserved, Iraq continued to be controlled by an authoritarian regime with a penchant for frightening its neighbors.

As is abundantly clear to anyone who watches television or reads the newspapers, the victory of the Gulf War did not produce a lasting solution to the region's problems. Instead, the war was only a prelude to round after round of additional violence. United States forces repeatedly launched air strikes against Iraqi targets in a frustrating effort to reduce Saddam Hussein's warmaking capabilities. Despite results that could be described, at best, as limited, our national administration continued to add to the list of targets for our air power. Within ten months in 1998 and 1999, we attacked not only Iraq but Afghanistan, Sudan and parts of the former Yugoslavia.

While the long-term results of these actions will not be ascertained with any certainty for a considerable period of time, few see any reason for jubilation and many feel a profound sense of frustration. The skill and courage of our armed forces, to say nothing of the expenditure of billions of dollars, has not succeeded in enforcing the vision of security outlined for the world by America's leaders. Once again we have been brought face to face with the fact that armed conflict rarely produces the glorious victories we see immortalized in statues and monuments. It may result in short-term success but, more often than not, the ultimate outcome of armed conflict is not victory but doubt, anxiety and intensified hostility.

Understanding the Limitations of Armed Force

Why is armed force seldom an effective instrument of national policy? For one thing, it cannot be used to resolve many of the complex political problems that are often the source of national concern and international tension. It is too costly, too inflexible and too risky to be employed to meet anything less than the most serious challenge to a nation's security. In addition, there is a tendency toward equilibrium on the battlefield. In Afghanistan, for example, the introduction of relatively inexpensive Stinger missiles gave a Mujahideen foot soldier the power to destroy a helicopter gunship worth millions of rubles.

In the present age of nuclear and other weapons of mass destruction, the limitations on military action are even more stringent. It is difficult to develop a scenario in which the benefits of a nuclear attack outweigh the negative consequences. There is simply no conceivable situation in which the national interests would be served by the utilization of even one of our thousands of nuclear devices.

Military commanders have long recognized that nuclear weapons serve no functional purpose on the battlefield. Their only conceivable use is as a deterrent against an attack by the nuclear weapons of another nation. Any other mission, especially any potential use of such weapons, would be a catastrophe. A weapon that can smash whole cities and incinerate millions of people is dysfunctional militarily and intolerable morally.

Impact of Technology

Technology has helped an increasing number of people understand that the use of military power is an outmoded concept. Through television, war has been brought into the living room. Ordinary citizens have seen what many of their leaders refuse to see—that armed force is counterproductive, that it yields only pain, death and the hatred that foments continuing conflict. The powerful images that are being transmitted around the world by television may be shaping public opinion that is skeptical of military action.

There is, of course, another side to the impact of television. It so inundates us with images of violence that it may have desensitized us to the ultimate violence of armed conflict. Television, as ubiquitous as it is compelling, may make it more difficult for viewers to separate fact from fiction. It may contribute to the skepticism and disbelief that often seem to characterize the thinking of many people in America and around the world.

Television coverage, like all reports of military action, also is subject to manipulation by those who have something to gain by attempting to put the best possible face on the inherent ugliness of war. When journalists are denied access to the field of action and television battle coverage is filtered through the military, as was the case during the Gulf War and subsequent military actions, we can expect less than objective reports and an exaggeration of the scope and significance of every successful operation.

While the influence of television on our thinking about war is open to debate, there is no debating the fact that technology has been quietly erasing the boundaries that traditionally separate nations. In recent years, barriers have been breaking down at an accelerating pace, creating for us a new world society or, more accurately, a one world society.

We can talk to people almost any place on earth in a matter of minutes. We can transmit a document across the country or a lunch order to the delicatessen down the street. Without leaving our homes, we can use the World Wide Web to collect information and exchange ideas. In a matter of hours, we can travel almost any place on earth. We can visit Europe or Asia more easily than America's founding fathers could visit a neighboring colony. We can witness distant events and have the sensation of being present at the events we witness. Technology has brought the people of the world together in ways that were unforeseen and perhaps unforeseeable a generation ago.

Clinging to the Military Myth

We are neighbors in a world community but we continue to have no certain way of protecting our lives and property from the world's burglars and bandits. We can put locks on our windows and doors. But we have not developed a foolproof system to get the criminals off our streets.

Of course, a great nation could use military force to attack the perceived source of the problem. But that would be like using a sledgehammer to smash a fly on a perfume bottle. Military action is by nature destructive and provocative. It carries with it the possibility that it will trigger a wider and deadlier conflict, a danger that most national leaders are unwilling to risk in this unsettled nuclear age.

Decades ago, President Dwight D. Eisenhower, no stranger to military affairs, pointed out that the quest for arms superiority can result in diminished security because it gives other nations an incentive to accelerate an arms build-up of their own. As the fall of the Soviet empire demonstrates, more armaments do not mean better defense or increased security and stability. They do signify a commitment to a mode of thinking that is outmoded and discredited.

Far too many leaders in the United States and abroad continue to cling to the military myth. They build their arsenals partly as a matter of misplaced national pride and partly because they remember that relationships within the world community traditionally have been conditioned by the existence of usable military force. So despite its obvious limitations and unmistakable obsolescence, it continues to be a major ingredient in the policy considerations of every nation.

If only world leaders would turn away from the past and start looking at the present and into the future, they might become aware of the worthlessness of the military alternative. It can only lead us onto a deadend road at a time when the world desperately needs a new road to its old dream of international security. It is the new road that we will follow in our search for the Fourth Freedom.

CHAPTER TWO

Our Place in Time and History

Opportunities are like sunrises. If you wait too long, you miss them.

—William Arthur Ward

We have reached great opportunity. Converging trends are conferring unprecedented responsibility and authority on the individual.

The evidence is unmistakable. For centuries, dictatorships in one form or another were the expected and accepted governmental system. Today dictators are an embattled rarity. They have been swept away by a devolution of power that has affected nations around the world. They are struggling to survive against a tide of democracy that is as powerful as it is irreversible.

With dictators in retreat and democracy on the rise, the door has opened. We can pursue our search for the Fourth Freedom with confidence and enthusiasm. The system we succeed in identifying will not be subject to arbitrary rejection by some unelected leader or unidentifiable counselor. It will be measured on the scale of common sense and judged by everyday individuals who share a determination to lift the fear of war from the minds and hearts of our children and grandchildren.

None of this was true when I first started chasing the dream of a lawful world. The door may not have been locked but it certainly wasn't open and the road outside seemed endlessly uphill. Dictatorships controlled many nations large and small. Relations among nations were frozen into Cold War patterns of behavior and preservation of the status quo seemed to be a permanent aspect of international affairs. The United States and the Soviet Union were in a state of perpetual, global confrontation. Some other nations, either freely or under duress, took sides with East or West. Still others tried to gain at least temporary advantage by selling their allegiance to the highest bidder.

In this dark environment, the possibility of capturing a dream seemed remote and my sense of frustration increased as I realized that two of the pillars of my approach were unlikely to receive universal acceptance. One of my pillars was the belief that economic power was the route to international security. The other was my certainty that the United States had to assume a take-charge role. As the world's paramount economic power, it had to exert responsible influence in the global arena.

With the superpowers continuing to invest huge sums in armaments, it seemed unrealistic to suppose they would recognize the value of cooperation. The culture of violence was too deeply rooted, the hostilities too great to expect the triumph of reason. And could I expect Soviet leaders to embrace a plan originated in the U.S. and, at least in its initial phases, dependent on U.S. power and authority? Denouncing the threat posed by America was the Soviet government's stock in trade. The Communist ruling elite helped maintain its grip on power through horror stories focusing on the great American bogeyman. U.S. leaders in turn were quick to blame the Soviets for every breakdown in international relations.

The obstacles clearly were great but, thanks to a combination of stubbornness and naiveté, I never lost my hope for the future. I persisted in my belief in the innate goodness of the world's people. Despite all the evidence to the contrary, I believed sanity was the normal human condition and that it eventually would be restored to the people who run the governments of the world. Given the prevailing atmosphere of East-West hostility, I was realistic enough to understand that neither Soviet nor American leaders were likely to embrace the nonviolent plan that was taking shape in my mind. But I never wavered in my belief that the obstacles to sanity would be overcome. Somehow, someway the dream of superpower cooperation would have to come true.

A Collapse that Rekindled Hope

Then to my amazement and applause, one of the most startling events in my lifetime started to unfold behind what Winston Churchill had described as "the Iron Curtain." Currents of unrest swept from the Baltic to the Bering. After decades of enforced uniformity and stifling secrecy, new patterns of thought and behavior began to emerge. Nikita Khrushchev cracked open the door to a closed society with a speech unmasking the evil of Joseph Stalin. Mikhail Gorbachev and others talked openly of a new role for public opinion. The words glasnost and perestroika entered the lexicon. But the reforms advocated by Gorbachev were too little and too late to preserve the dominance of his own Communist Party or the empire it had ruled for seven decades.

In Russia and in the nations newly freed from Kremlin control, democracy was replacing totalitarianism. Market-driven economies were shattering the stagnation of state planning and state control. The rule of law was pushing aside generations of despotism and timeless traditions of spirituality were experiencing a rebirth. Of course, there were problems. Economic insecurity created new fears and doubts. Crime threatened the safety of ordinary citizens and uncertainty became a dominating theme in conversations in every community and every home. But the flame of hope was burning more brightly than anyone could remember and millions of people were coming to believe their dream of peace and opportunity could come true.

The earthshaking events that transformed Eastern and Central Europe were largely nonviolent. In nation after nation, unarmed people walked unafraid into the streets and with their courage, determination and idealism, they changed the world. They helped create a climate of positive expectations in which, despite disappointments and difficulties, the dream of freedom was realized.

With the collapse of the Soviet empire came unprecedented progress toward arms reduction. In the initial years of the post–Cold War era, many of the nations that emerged from Soviet domination began to adopt the principles of a nonmilitary approach to international security. Weapons of mass destruction and armaments expenditures were reduced. Trade with the United States and other industrialized democracies increased. Especially in Central Europe, nations began to taste the benefits of full participation in the enriching mainstream of international commerce. The door opened to greater prosperity and security.

Limitations of Arms Reduction Negotiations

The progress achieved in the post–Cold War era went way beyond the meager results of previous arms control negotiations. During the Cold War, each new round of talks seemed to be followed by the introduction of additional and more devastating weapons. The bomber-dropped A-bomb of 1945 was transformed into multiple warheads carried by missiles that can be launched from a continent away or from the hidden depths of the ocean. Diplomats talked of peace while the arms industry built new instruments of destruction.

This tendency should have come as no surprise. It is as old as human history. It reflects an obvious fact: When people meet to negotiate, they seek not to weaken their relative position but to strengthen it. Negotiators in arms limitations talks represent constituencies that will not tolerate any concession that could be interpreted as a retreat. They are too wary of each other, too doubtful of the other's intentions. As a result, arms limitations talks in the Cold War era seemed to have been most useful as platforms for propaganda and incubators for new generations of more destructive weapons.

Successful Steps toward Denuclearization

This is not to say there has been no progress. Arms reduction agreements made when political enmity disappeared at the end of the Cold War produced very worthwhile results. Important steps were taken on the road to denuclearization and a safer world. The Intermediate Nuclear Force (INF) Treaty of 1988 did away with an entire class of nuclear weapons in Europe. The 1991 and 1993 START treaties significantly reduced the number of long-range nuclear warheads. The Nuclear non-Proliferation Treaty, negotiated in 1968 to slow the spread of nuclear weapons, was permanently extended in 1995. The Comprehensive Test Ban Treaty prohibited all nuclear explosions. The Conventional Forces in

Europe (CFE) Treaty greatly reduced the type and number of conventional weapons in Europe.

Taken together, these arms limitation treaties demonstrate the willingness of nations to pull back from an embrace with global death. Nations have reduced the size of their arsenals of mass destruction and have revealed their willingness to make even deeper reductions. Now the governments of the world must be brought to the realization that the time is right to take a giant step forward by systematically eliminating all of the weapons that threaten humanity and its future.

The Fatal Flaw in Arms Treaties

When you carefully examine arms control agreements of the past, you realize that they are seriously limited by their lack of a mechanism that will assure compliance. They are subject to changing interpretations that may be proclaimed by a new generation of leaders. They are not part of a comprehensive system designed to provide lasting, global protection from weapons of mass destruction.

In many ways, arms control talks are an easy way out for national leaders. By sitting down to negotiate, they can project an image of rationality. They can appear to be striving to eliminate the threat of nuclear war. Yet, at the same time, they can avoid the hard decisions—and the risk—involved in seeking a sound and lasting solution to the problem. The situation has much in common with that of a patient who has been told of a life-threatening cancer. If the cancer is surgically removed, the patient has a very good chance of making a complete recovery and living a normal life. But the operation is difficult and involves an element of risk. The patient is concerned about the operation and begins a frantic search for a risk-free alternative. With luck, the patient will abandon the search and consent to surgery before it is too late. But if the search is prolonged, if the cancer is allowed to spread, death is a certainty.

The cancer of nuclear, biological and chemical arms has been spreading for more than five decades and the supposed remedy of arms agreements has been an aspirin, not a cure. Past limitations agreements have created a sense of well-being by reducing the patient's temperature a degree or two but they have not eliminated the fundamental problem that produced the fever in the first place. To a large degree, they have been based on national expediency, not the rule of law. Arms reduction negotiations may have given the world a false sense of security. They may have lulled people into believing that the life or death problem of nuclear weapons can be solved through unenforceable treaties that nations may violate whenever it appears to be in their best interest.

Why would any nation—or any individual, for that matter—abide by an agreement when it provides cosmetic rather than real benefits? Why should we accept a system lacking a means of penalizing violators? When a toothless treaty is violated by one nation, the other nation responds with a violation of its own. In the case of nuclear weapons, even if negotiations continue to bring about a reduction in numbers, the danger of accidental or intended catastrophe would remain.

Dramatic Reductions Are Vital

If nuclear arsenals were reduced by 50 percent, and I fervently wish this would happen immediately, there would still be enough weapons to kill every person on earth several times over. If the reduction reached 95 percent, the United States and the Russian Federation, the two principal members of the nuclear club, would continue to each possess hundreds of thermonuclear devices, every one of them many times more powerful than the bomb dropped on Hiroshima.

With a 95 percent reduction in the nuclear arsenals of the U.S. and Russia—a decrease not foreseen by even the most optimistic observers of the arms reduction process—the world still would be faced with a threat far beyond that which existed when the nuclear age dawned. And this does not include the nuclear weapons stockpiled by Britain, France, China and the other acknowledged or clandestine nuclear powers.

For those concerned about the survival of civilization, a threat of such magnitude ought to be totally unacceptable. Indeed, there is no such thing as an acceptable level of nuclear or any other weapons of mass destruction. As long as there is a single nuclear weapon or a single canister of biological or chemical poison, there is no guarantee that it will not be detonated or activated with appalling consequences. Whether there are two or 2,000 nuclear weapons, ten or 10,000 bombs packed with biological toxins or chemical contaminants, we have two choices. We can tolerate the situation and accept continued danger or we can move in new and productive ways to end the threat once and for all.

Leadership and Cooperation Can Produce Results

When Presidents Bush and Gorbachev acted in 1991 to reduce the number of so-called tactical nuclear weapons deployed on either side of what once had been the Iron Curtain, negotiations were almost non existent. Yet, the Bush–Gorbachev initiatives resulted in the withdrawal or dismantlement of 13,000 nuclear weapons, the largest single act of denuclearization in history. To produce such a positive outcome, each leader acted on his own to reduce the risk, and the result was a triumph for international security and common sense. By this action, Presidents Bush and Gorbachev demonstrated that much can be achieved through leadership and cooperation. They showed that there is no need to rely on negotiations that take far more time than the world has to spare.

Retired Admiral Stansfield Turner has made the same point in his important book, *Caging the Nuclear Genie* (Westview, 1997). Arms reduction can be achieved most effectively through presidential leadership. Elaborate arms control negotiations often delay and dilute the weapons reduction process. The additional challenge of gaining legislative ratification can create further roadblocks.

It also should be clear that agreements lacking mechanisms for enforcement have about as much substance as the emperor's new suit of clothes. An unenforceable agreement is not only worthless, it is dangerous. It fosters deception and duplicity and it distracts from coming to grips with life-and-death issues. It keeps us from focusing on an ancient, honorable and attainable goal, peace based on international law.

Growing Acceptance of the Rule of Law

The global extension of the rule of law is an inevitable consequence of the realities of today's world. Much progress already has been made. In his book, *A Common Sense Guide to World Peace* (Oceania Publications, Inc., New York, New York, 1985), Professor Benjamin B. Ferencz points out many encouraging examples of the strengthening of international law. "The number of nations joining cooperative international efforts has been consistently increasing," said Professor Ferencz. "Each advance— though inadequate—was an improvement on the past. The line of progress is there for all to see."

Professor Ferencz lists such developments as the United Nations Convention on the Law of the Sea, agreements on the exploration and utilization of outer space, cooperation in the battle against hunger and disease through such agencies as the World Health Organization and, interestingly, promotion and control of nonmilitary use of atomic energy through the International Atomic Energy Agency. Nations voluntarily ratified these agreements because they perceived them to be in their own best interests. Their willingness to take such action indicates a growing awareness of the importance of the rule of law in international affairs.

Positive Influence of the UN

Since 1990, the UN has been at the center of even more ambitious cooperative efforts to solve international problems. Nations have worked together to lessen disease and starvation in Africa, reduce the human suffering and insecurity triggered by the break-up of the former Yugoslavia, roll back aggression by Iraq, assure compliance by Iraq, North Korea and other states with international weapons agreements and monitor elections in Haiti, El Salvador and other locations. The UN Security Council has also approved the imposition of sanctions against nations that have been perceived to be in violation of international standards of good behavior.

During the same post–Cold War period, the UN also has had its share of fumbled opportunities. It failed to act promptly to stop genocide in Yugoslavia and, for the most part, it turned its back on even more deadly genocidal behavior in Africa. It was tepid in its response to religious and ethnic persecution, the threat of state-sponsored terrorism and the violations of international order committed by Libya, Sudan and other nations. But given the limitations of the present UN system, the organization has taken important strides in making the world a safer place.

Need for Mandatory Compliance

There is, of course, one obvious difference between what the UN has been able to accomplish and the peacekeeping system we are striving to identify and construct. The UN now depends on voluntary involvement and voluntary compliance. The system we must put in place will assure compliance with antiaggression, antiweapons law through an institutionalized system of rewards and penalties. Such a system—and the law it will enforce—are logical steps in the evolutionary development of the international rule of law.

The law banning aggression and weapons of mass destruction deals with the most serious of subjects—the survival of life itself. It cannot be equated with rules governing less serious matters. For example, regulations focusing on the collection of minerals from the ocean floor may well be left to voluntary compliance. The law safeguarding our planet from destruction cannot be an optional matter. It must be universally accepted and rigorously enforced.

One World Is a Reality

In nearly every conceivable way, the nations of earth have moved well beyond the days of imaginary self-sufficiency. In communication and transportation, for example, satellites assist the navigators of air and ocean, broadcast radio and television signals to and from the most distant locations and provide the connections that enable human beings—and the computers human beings have created—to talk across the miles.

Technology has knocked down the walls between nations, facilitating an accelerating exchange of information. The flow is so powerful, its potential benefits so great, that it is beyond resistance. It penetrated the traditional insularity of the Soviet Union, shook the leadership of the People's Republic of China, created a climate of expectation in Africa and Latin America and suggested the fulfillment of Wendell Willkie's

World War II prophecy of One World. In a world without islands—the "global village" described by Marshall McLuhan—global law is a necessity. Law is the only assurance of justice, the only barrier against violence and oppression. Law offers the only reliable hope of taking the gun out of the hand of the aggressor, ending the threat of war and preserving the earth and its people.

The prize of peace through international agreement in the form of law is so desirable that it is difficult to understand why it repeatedly has slipped through humanity's fingers. The high hopes of the past—from the Hague Conventions to the League of Nations to the United Nations—have not been realized. Treaties that supposedly have the force of law have been signed, sealed and ignored. Aggressive military action continues to be the prerogative of any nation. Without an effective mechanism for judging a nation's actions and a means of enforcing the judgment, how could it be otherwise?

Why We Must Establish the Rule of Law

In a world without a universally accepted international judicial or enforcement system, no nation will risk its independence on the strength of a piece of paper and a handshake. National leaders will not jeopardize the safety of their fellow citizens—and their own careers—by gambling on the sincerity of their counterparts across the frontier. Asking the nations of the world to base the elimination of weapons of mass destruction solely on a foundation of mutual trust is as utopian as asking a family to entrust the safety of its home and possessions to the goodwill of a population that inevitably includes a burglar or two. The family quite wisely will prefer to rely on the rule of law, backed by the defense of a sturdy lock and an effective police force. The family knows that enforceable law provides the framework in which trust can operate. What is true for a family is equally true for the family of nations.

Once this fundamental fact of human relationships is understood, it is apparent what must be done. Humanity must discover a way to guarantee agreements between sovereign states. Humanity must create an environment that encourages trust among nations and a system that provides ironclad assurance against aggression.

Concentrating on the Fundamental Issue

The development of such a system surely is not beyond the capacity of the human mind. The problem is that some of our best minds have been concentrating on the perpetuation of nuclear terror. They have been planning and building weapons, theorizing about the desirability of first or second strike strategies, arguing about what is rather than what might be. They have ignored the fundamental issue of building lasting international security.

Soon after World War II, civic leader Basil O'Connor warned, "The world cannot continue to wage war like physical giants and to seek peace like intellectual pygmies." It is a warning the world must heed. We must mobilize our intellectual resources in the cause of peace. We must break the constraining bonds of the past and begin thinking in terms of the future. Without surrendering national identities, we must create a program that will lead to the supremacy of world law, a program that must result in the establishment of a powerful, yet humane, system of enforcement, including civil and criminal courts that are accepted, respected and obeyed. Such a system must be based on a force that is stronger than military power, upon which armed might itself depends: The force of economic power.

The United States, in cooperation with other nations, possesses or controls vast economic resources that can be utilized in the creation and enforcement of an international law that will effectively eliminate aggression and weapons of mass destruction. Despite the lawlessness revealed by America's regrettable flirtation with the role of international policeman, we have a tradition of belief in the law. We respect the importance of the individual. We believe in ourselves and in the future. We have faith in the institutions we have developed. Unfortunately, the strength of our optimism sometimes has been a handicap. In the field of international relationships, it has blinded us to the peril all of us face.

But while the peril is real, so is the opportunity that today presents itself. We have been given a chance to seek out a practical solution to the problems created by the world's addiction to weapons of mass destruction. We must have the courage to proceed.

CHAPTER THREE

Discovering the Reality of Power

Justice and power must be brought together so that whatever is just may be powerful and whatever is powerful may be just.

—Pascal

Power is not inherently evil. In itself, power is neither good nor bad. It is a necessary element for the functioning of any society. It is wishful thinking to believe that international security can be achieved without employing power. But for power to be useful and effective, it must be kept under control. Gasoline burning in the open is wasteful and potentially destructive. Gasoline burning in the controlled environment of an engine yields power that can be harnessed to produce positive results.

Physical force and power are not the same. They do not equate. Physical force, which includes military force, is only one of many kinds of power. In fact, in the hierarchy of power, physical force is far less persuasive than two other forms of power, the power of the word and the power of economics.

Of these three forms of power, I believe the power of the word is the most potent. If it is employed in the service of good, it nourishes the human spirit, fosters faith, unleashes the imagination and stimulates the vision that is the starting point for all human achievement. If it is employed in the service of evil, it poisons the human spirit, destroys faith, stifles the imagination and dims the vision of what we are and what we can become. The power of the word can lift men and women to higher levels of fulfillment or it can condemn them to hatred, frustration and failure.

The power of the word is most effective in influencing behavior because it acknowledges the supremacy of the spiritual side of human nature. On the other hand, economic power can only deal with the secular side of human affairs. Even so, it is far more persuasive than physical force. Economic power can achieve goals well beyond the reach of all the armies of the world.

Power to Give and to Withhold

In its simplest terms, economic power is the power to give and to withhold. It is universal in character, politically and ideologically neutral and eminently practical. It provides for our physical needs and serves as a primary tool for the improvement of our condition. Economic exchange is part of the lives of all of us. We are experienced in giving and withholding. We know that incentives and sanctions, carrots and sticks, are used in diplomacy at all levels, from the family and the community to international affairs. With international trade growing at a dramatic rate, economic power is playing an increasingly important role on the global stage. It is binding nations together, enabling them to take advantage of their strengths and compensate for their weaknesses. It is creating opportunities to develop new and effective ways of achieving international security.

Given the interdependent economies of today's international community, it is easy to see why the economic tools of statecraft, incentives and sanctions, are being used with increased frequency and success. These tools can diminish the threat of global destruction and enforce the rule of law in international affairs. The power of economics has the ability to free the world's people from fear of the awesome weapons that have been accumulated in a fruitless pursuit of international security. The power of economics, the power to give or to withhold, can induce nations to freely and gratefully accept the rule of law. It also can effectively punish criminal national leaders, those who use the power of their offices to disrupt society through aggression and repression. The power of economics is far more flexible than military force. Economic weapons can be employed in a far wider variety of difficult situations than can the weapons of war. Besides, economic power is far less likely to create the kind of violent reaction that is the usual result of military action.

Withholding Has Proven Its Effectiveness

The power to withhold is so frequently used, so natural, so much a part of our daily lives that we rarely acknowledge its importance. In a way, it is like the sun. We know the sun exists but we don't stop to think of it as the source of the energy that fuels our earth. We know that the power to give and withhold exists, but we don't stop to consider that this power can influence our transactions with others, creating the conditions that shape our lives.

Individuals, organizations and governments use the power to withhold every day to effect change, improve conditions, exercise control or gain an advantage. A parent withholds privileges from an unruly child. Consumers withhold purchases to influence the behavior of manufacturers or retailers. Employees withhold their labor from employers to improve working conditions or wages. Governments withhold money, privileges and freedom to obtain compliance with their laws and maintain their ascendancy. Both physical force and withholding can be used to improve a situation. But there is a profound difference in the way they are used and in the effect they have on those who use them and on those they are used against.

Inherent in the use of physical force is the reaction of those against whom it is used, a reaction directed against the users. This reaction can be so strong and so violent that it eliminates all the gains that force was supposed to achieve. As we know from history, war sows the seeds of future conflict, creating hostilities that extend from generation to generation.

Utilizing both Carrot and Stick

On the other hand, withholding is nonviolent and rarely produces a violent reaction. Withholding achieves the desired results because implied in its use is the ability to give. Physical force totally lacks this ability. It can take away but it cannot give. The power to withhold is effective because it has positive as well as negative attributes. It works because it involves the possibility of transferring something desirable from one party to another. It incorporates both the carrot and the stick. Physical force, on the other hand, is one-dimensional. It is entirely negative. It is incapable of providing rewards. It offers no carrot, only a stick. If the stick fails to produce results, physical force has only one answer: Get a bigger stick.

The ability to give, inherent in the power to withhold, makes possible successful agreements, treaties and laws. All of these are, in essence, contracts between two or more parties. A contract is successful when it benefits all parties that are involved. A contract that does this will endure. A contract that is unfair because it favors one party over another—a likely occurrence when a contract is negotiated at gunpoint—is almost certain to create more problems than benefits, even for the favored party. The party that is less favored almost always will seek to violate the agreement by any means, fair or foul.

Because so many of the world's leaders—and private citizens as well—seem to be locked into outmoded and crippling habits of thought, the power of economics rarely has been given a fair chance to serve as a substitute for military power. When we think about power in the context of international affairs, military force continues to come to mind. We customarily rank nations according to their military capabilities. Wasn't it Stalin who, in a discussion of world opinion, scornfully asked, "How many divisions does the Pope have?" Had he lived, Stalin would have seen that hundreds of divisions could not save the Soviet empire from collapsing under the weight of its economic inadequacies and the demand of its people for the human dignity espoused by, among others, the Pope.

Despite this telling example, we are so conditioned by militaristic thinking that we speak of powers and superpowers in accordance with the number of divisions they have in the field and the size of their nuclear and conventional arsenals. We know from experience that we're living in a violent world and we tend to be skeptical about nonviolent solutions to the world's problems.

Economic Power Solves Problems Every Day

But day after day we work out our own problems without resort to violence. We applaud laws aimed at violent offenders. We abhor all forms of destructive behavior. We want to live our lives among civilized adults, not adolescent bullies. We acknowledge that economic power has a profound influence on our daily existence. We negotiate for a raise in pay or a promotion to a position more suitable to our talents and interests. We use economic power to influence our politicians. Within our families, we rely on economic power to instruct or discipline our children and to maintain peace in our households.

Economic power is an old and trusted friend. It is part of our daily lives. Why are we reluctant to give it more of a role in international security? Why have we been unable to understand that economic power, not military force, is the key that will unlock the door to a more peaceful tomorrow?

Part of our problem flows from our perception of what has, or has not, happened when nonviolent solutions have been attempted. For example, the United States, the world's greatest economic power, has been frustrated in many of its attempts to exercise nonviolent power in pursuit of what it perceives as its national objectives. The reason for the frustration is not the idea of using economic power but the flawed nature of U.S. efforts to implement the idea, to utilize its economic resources to influence the course of international events.

Unilateral Sanctions Usually Fail

The United States has lacked a consistent and comprehensive plan. It has tended to use its economic power unilaterally. It has not always created the multilateral unity that ought to be an essential element in the utilization of economic power in diplomacy. Without the support of the major trading nations, primary sanctions against violators of international order are not likely to succeed and secondary sanctions aimed at those who trade with the violators have no chance of success whatsoever.

The United States has withheld trade from violators but, without the support of other major trading nations and without international agreement on the necessity of both primary and secondary sanctions, violators often have been able to shrug their shoulders at a U.S. embargo. They know they can find another source for the goods they need.

Our Cuban Experience

Cuba is an instructive example. When Fidel Castro established his one-party dictatorship, identified himself as a committed Communist and put his nation under the patronage of the Soviet Union, the United States responded with a trade embargo. At the time of Castro's ascendancy, 75 percent of Cuba's trade was with the United States. But the Cubans quickly shifted it to the Soviet Union and its allies, all but eliminating the effect of the U.S. embargo. In addition, the Soviets provided economic assistance in the range of $2 billion to $3 billion per year.

Then came the upheaval in Eastern Europe. When the Soviet Union collapsed, the subsidy to Cuba disappeared and so did much of Cuba's trade with what had been the Soviet bloc. But other nations, including many of America's closest friends, filled the trade gap. When the U.S. strengthened its sanctions in 1996, Cuba's new trading partners objected strenuously. The U.S. embargo, undertaken with the best of intentions, ended up as a source of tension with our friends without seeming to move Cuba even a half-step closer to democratic reform.

Sanctions Must Apply to both Lawbreakers and Accomplices

It seems to me that this experience should have taught two lessons. The first is that unilateral economic sanctions rarely produce the desired results. They may make us feel good or satisfy the demands of some domestic voting bloc, but they lack the scope and authority to have serious impact on the targeted nation. The second lesson is that if the United States and other nations are serious about utilizing nonviolent power in the international arena, the act of withholding cannot be limited to a single target. It must include both violators of international law *and their accomplices. Trade must be withheld from nations that are threats to security and from their trading partners as well.*

Some object to the idea of extending sanctions to include both lawbreakers and nations trading with lawbreakers. The objectors say the sanctioning of accomplices will disrupt political and other vital relationships and create new and more complex sets of problems. For example, say the objectors, if we imposed economic sanctions on Canada because it continued to trade with Cuba, wouldn't we run the risk of alienating one of our oldest and closest trading partners and allies? Could we expect a sanctioned Canada to cooperate with us in regulating North Atlantic fishing or in cracking down on smuggling?

This objection would be valid except for two considerations. First, sanctions imposed by one nation against another rarely succeed and, as I have pointed out, should never be attempted. Second, if sanctions are applied only for serious offenses rather than minor infractions of international law or because of differences in ideology or culture or religious belief, they will have broader international support. My focus is on the ultimate crimes against global order and security—armed aggression, the possession of weapons of mass destruction, the fostering of terrorism and the commission of genocide. Given the enormity of such crimes, why should we, or the world for that matter, worry about the possibility of hurt national feelings or the niceties of international politics? Why wouldn't all nations of goodwill unite in imposing penalties that would punish criminal conduct and vindicate the rule of law?

Self-Interest Must Yield to World Interest

We also need to adjust some of our thinking about the U.S. role in world affairs. We have to understand that self-interest and world interest are not always identical. We must realize that we can be most effective when we put aside self-interest and act in behalf of the interests of the world community. In the long run, this broader vision will pay major dividends to the United States. It will create unprecedented opportunities for our human and material resources. It will enable us to exercise constructive leadership in a global society that has been granted new hope of achieving its potential.

It's also worth noting that the United States, like many other nations, has tended to emphasize sanctions rather than inducements, punishment rather than rewards. Americans and their leaders seem to forget that some of the greatest triumphs of U.S. foreign policy came when we utilized our ability to give.

Helping Enemies to Their Feet

After World War II, we gave our wealth in the rebuilding of Western Europe, including support for nations that had been our principal European enemies. In so doing, we achieved major foreign policy objectives. We cultivated a fertile seedbed for democracy. We created an obstacle to the westward territorial ambitions of the Soviet Union. We established a robust trading partner, one that has been a major, consistent market for our goods and services, a source of products for our economy and a competitive force that has stimulated innovation and productivity in American business. Our leadership and generosity helped spark the development of a community of nations so strong and prosperous that its very existence contributed to the end of the Soviet bloc.

When the Soviet Union dissolved, Germany stepped forward with a substantial package of economic assistance that accelerated the withdrawal of Soviet troops from Eastern Europe. As with the Marshall Plan in Europe and the enlightened U.S. policies that undergirded the rebuilding of Japan, Germany's action illustrates what can be accomplished through incentives. In these cases, nations helped former enemies get to their feet again and, with Germany and Japan, the military threat they once posed has been eliminated.

For the U.S.: Special Opportunities and Responsibilities

Today we must deal not only with nations that have been defeated militarily but with nations that have been defeated economically. We must develop a cohesive strategy that will work to reduce international tensions and focus world attention on the urgency of nuclear, biological and chemical disarmament. America's foreign policy must be based on honesty and openness. It must treat all nations with fairness in the certain belief that the every day people of all nations are basically good and well intentioned. We must never lose sight of the fundamental goodness of people, even those who are the citizens of nations with bad governments and evil policies. Then we will implement a plan based on the mobilization of the power of trade—incentives and sanctions, the carrot and the stick.

There is much recent evidence that such a plan will work. Economic incentives played a critical role in inducing Ukraine to divest itself of the 2,000-plus nuclear weapons left on its soil when the Soviet Union disappeared. The destruction of these weapons, a significant step toward nuclear disarmament, teaches a basic lesson: The danger posed by weapons of mass destruction can be reduced through the prudent use of economic power. Why cannot this power be used in support of international law banning aggression and outlawing weapons of mass destruction? Why cannot the power of trade be used to protect the people of all nations by diminishing enmity, ending aggression and fostering understanding, cooperation and mutual concern?

As the world's largest trading nation and the leader of the world's democratic industrialized nations, the United States has a special opportunity and a special responsibility. It is in a unique position to use its economic power for good. Through our ability to offer or withhold trade, we can enlist the support of our trading partners. We can persuade a majority of the world's nations to join in building the consensus that is the first step in the creation of an enforceable international law dealing with the problems of aggression and mass destruction. Such law would meet the test of fairness and provide equal protection to all. It would be welcomed by every nation that values the right of its people to be free from fear.

Power to Usher in an Age of Lasting Security

Should the United States fail to provide leadership in utilizing its nonviolent power in the cause of peace, should our economic power be wasted on narrow self-interest and our energies dissipated in the expansion of our war-making capabilities and in the fruitless pursuit of unenforceable international agreements, the opportunity to create lasting and genuine global security could be lost forever.

The leadership of the United States is vital to the success of our search for the Fourth Freedom. By facing up to the reality of today's world and accepting our responsibility for shaping this period of human history, Americans can exert a powerful positive influence on the world and its future. *If we will change the way we think about power, we will be well on our way to discovering a system that will guarantee a truly lawful world.*

CHAPTER FOUR

Why the U.S. Must Lead

God and the politicians willing, the United States can declare peace upon the world and win it.

—Eli Culbertson

During my personal journey in search of the Fourth Freedom, I repeatedly was surprised by the reaction of more than a handful of well-informed, intelligent Americans. They listened politely as I outlined some of my thoughts. Sometimes they even nodded their approval. But when I asked for their objections, they immediately focused on my belief that the United States has a special responsibility to provide global leadership.

Some of the objectors were motivated by the isolationism that always has been a factor in the thinking of many Americans. They not only want to, as the bumper sticker puts it, "Get the U.S. out of the UN," they would be delighted if our country could somehow cut itself off from all the rest of the world.

Exploring Objections to a U.S. Leadership Role

This, of course, is impossible. We cannot turn our backs on other countries and other peoples. Like it or not, we are inescapably linked to them and the linkage is growing stronger every day. It is creating opportunities for us and for them. Our involvement in the global economy and in international affairs is paying dividends to us and to our neighbors everywhere.

Nonetheless, I respect the motives of many of those who say they want America to turn its back to the world. For the most part, they are driven by their belief that America is the greatest country in history. They fear that commitments beyond our borders ultimately will destroy the nation they love. While I do not believe their fears are justified, their patriotism stands in refreshing contrast to the cynicism and doubt that characterize the thinking of others. These Americans, including some who hold positions of great responsibility and influence, have a negative view of the role the United States has played in international affairs since the end of World War II. They tend to blame the U.S. for most of the world's problems or, at the very least, they lump together the U.S. and its enemies as moral equivalents, equally to blame for all the postwar rivalries that have had a serious negative impact on society as a whole. These Americans maintain that the United States has no right to attempt to influence other nations, that it has no monopoly on goodness or wisdom and that it should let its global neighbors make up their own minds without inducements or sanctions.

Still others reject the thought of special responsibility for the U.S. on the grounds that it would imply an admission of guilt for the role our country played in the development and use of nuclear weapons. These objectors—and they well may be speaking for a majority of Americans—do not feel the U.S. owes the world an apology or anything else.

Judging the U.S. Record

My own view is that our country's responsibility is self-evident, not because of any feelings of guilt, but because U.S. leadership long has had a profoundly positive influence on world affairs. Admittedly, the United States sometimes has blundered and fumbled in its relationships with other nations. More than once over the years, it has lost its way. It has failed to live up to the expectations of its people and the people of other nations. Worst of all, from time to time it has forgotten the principles that guided its founding and undergirded its progress.

But it seems to me that the record of history mainly shows that the United States is simply a very human country. It has all the vices and virtues of the individual human being. It can be meek and arrogant, understanding and inconsiderate, generous and stingy. It can demonstrate its love for peace and, occasionally, its eagerness to throw its weight around. But as with an individual, a nation should not be judged according to some rigorous formula for calculating its virtues and vices. It should be judged on the sum total of its influence on society.

In the case of the United States, I believe it will come through such a judgment with flying colors. Any objective review of the past will show that over the years the United States has set an admirable standard of behavior. Americans have been reluctant to become involved in war and, for the most part, they have resisted the temptation to use military power to expand America's territory.

Where Would the World Be without the U.S.?

At the same time, they have created a society that enjoys the admiration of much of the world. While we may believe that many aspects of American life today reflect a decline in standards, our country remains the world's best example of what freedom can achieve. America is not blameless in either domestic policy or foreign affairs. But those who question U.S. responsibility to provide leadership ought to ask themselves: What would the world be like if the United States had never existed?

Depending on personal perspectives and individual experiences, each person undoubtedly will have a different answer. But I am confident that many of these answers will be built around the fundamental themes of freedom and diversity. For more than two centuries, the United States has provided the world with a lesson in what can be accomplished through a commitment to the freedom of the individual. This commitment has fostered healthy competition, stimulated social and economic initiatives and built a society that, for all of its imperfections, remains the model for most of the rest of the world.

Freedom's Attraction and Benefits

From the very beginning of the American experience, our country's commitment to freedom has attracted the homeless, the hungry and the oppressed of other countries. It has lured to our shores innovators and idealists, artists and intellectuals. It has been a magnet to men and women of many cultures, to all who share a desire to make up their own minds about what is in their own best interest. This commitment to freedom has contributed to U.S. economic strength, created a voluntary sector that is as important as it is unique and encouraged the establishment of religious and educational institutions that satisfy the widest range of spiritual and educational needs.

All of these accomplishments of our freedom-driven society have been watched and emulated by most of the rest of the world. When the freedom of other countries was in jeopardy, when threats needed to be answered, when injustices needed to be corrected, the world knew it could count on the United States. Its citizens fought wars to preserve the freedom of others and, in the post–World War II period, American taxpayers built and maintained a powerful military machine to defend the cause of freedom around the world.

America has handed to the world a shining example of productive diversity. Americans have demonstrated that people of differing backgrounds, beliefs and attainments can live together in a lasting and mutually beneficial relationship. They have shown that diversity can enrich a nation, that ethnic, cultural, religious and other differences can serve to strengthen a society—if that society understands and accepts both the importance of the individual and the supremacy of law.

World's Number One Market

As the world's leading trading nation and the leader of democratic, industrialized society, the United States maintains unquestioned economic leadership. Despite its substantial federal debt and its worrisome trade deficit, it remains far and away the number one economic power. The U.S. economy is roughly twice the size of Japan's and we are number one in both imports and exports.

During the past few years, the U.S. consistently has created more new jobs than Japan and Western Europe combined. More Americans are employed than ever before and they are using their paychecks to buy more things, including the products of other nations. Their pocketbook power reinforces the position of the United States as the world's most desirable market.

The appetite of Americans for such products as automobiles, telephones, electronic equipment, light bulbs, office machines, furniture and wearing apparel is so strong it has attracted the attention of marketeers from around the world. The nations of the European Union as well as Japan, China, Korea, Eastern Europe, Africa, Latin America and every other part of the globe are eager to compete for a share of our purchases.

Exporting Agricultural, Manufactured and Information Products

On the production side of the ledger, the agricultural sector of the American economy ranks first in the export of raw or processed corn, soybeans, wheat, cotton, and other products. American industry leads in exporting aircraft, computers, data-processing equipment, and a variety of other types of machinery and equipment, including, it should be noted, nuclear reactors. In this information age, the U.S. is far and away the leader in information technology. It is the preeminent source of the software that governs the computers that control the world's financial, commercial, governmental, and other institutions. It is the principal incubator for the computer-related ideas that are accelerating the world's rush into the next century.

In manufacturing, the business segment with which I am most familiar, American companies are more than holding their own against overseas competitors. U.S. manufacturing productivity has been rising steadily and, to assure continuing improvement, U.S. business is increasing its spending on new plants and equipment. The climate for profitable manufacturing in the U.S. is so favorable that foreign companies, including many headquartered in Germany and Japan, are choosing to make substantial investments in production facilities in America.

One Company's Global Success

I know from personal experience that American ingenuity is unsurpassed. Without bragging or boasting, I can say that the agriculture-related products manufactured by CTB, Inc., the company I founded, are among the very best the world has to offer. That's why it has grown from a modest facility in a small town in northern Indiana into a worldwide business that markets its products in more than 100 countries. Its overseas success has improved conditions in other parts of the world and created jobs back home. Its experience, like the experience of other companies across America, demonstrates that access to the world marketplace plays a powerful, positive role in expanding the U.S. economy.

In this age of a one-world economy, national interests and global interests are the same. Businesses have found that to prosper locally, they must compete globally. They must overcome the temptation of protectionism and welcome the opportunities created by global competition. As consumers, we do not hesitate to purchase Japanese electronic goods or Chinese wearing apparel. We are globalists in the way we live our lives. We must become globalists in our thinking about America's relations with other nations.

Mass Media's Role in Shaping Our Thinking

Perhaps part of the problem is the fact that much of the business news transmitted to the American people does not paint a very upbeat picture. More attention is given to U.S. economic problems—real and imagined—than to its countless economic achievements. If the stock market takes even a minor dip, business reporters seek the opinions of analysts bent on predicting impending disaster. If a company lays off part of its workforce, it is likely to be given headline treatment on television and in newspapers. If it expands employment, its action is likely to be ignored by television and relegated to the obituary page in the newspaper. As a result, many Americans have an inaccurate, negative view of the strength of their economy. They do not realize that they are participating in the most powerful economic system in world history, a system that is producing unprecedented wealth and opportunity.

Ironically, the mass media that often has failed to give Americans an accurate account of the strength of their economy long has been the messenger of America's richness to the citizens of other lands. Jack Valenti, a veteran spokesman for America's motion picture industry, has pointed out that even films that present a negative view of American life can have a positive influence in other parts of the world. He cites as an example the vintage film, *The Grapes of Wrath*. While Americans were distressed by the film's painful portrayal of Dust Bowl poverty in the 1930s, many non-Americans were impressed to learn from the film that in America even some of the poorest families own their own automobiles.

America: Economic Role Model

American affluence, projected by television and films into distant homes and meeting places, continues to attract a steady stream of immigrants from around the world. They want to take advantage of the opportunities, to make their dreams of financial security come true. They seek to follow in the footsteps of the millions of other immigrants whose talents, energy and determination have enabled them to attain the highest levels of personal achievement and, at the same time, make a lasting contribution to America's economic success.

Even those who stay at home have been influenced by the power of the American model. Hong Kong, Singapore, Taiwan and South Korea owe much to the American economic example. So do Brazil, Chile, Mexico and other Latin American nations. In Eastern Europe, the nations of the former Soviet bloc are eager for information on how American skill, knowledge, and experience have created an economy that can enrich every level of society.

Even the People's Republic of China, one of the few countries that continues to pay lip service to centralized Marxist economic theory, has been moving toward private economic initiatives based on the American pattern. Without publicly admitting the scope of its reforms, China is accepting many elements of a market-oriented individual incentive system and the growth of China's economy, especially the export sector, indicates that its flirtation with capitalism is producing rewards.

Primacy of America's Popular Culture

China, like even the most remote countries on earth, also has been influenced—for better or worse—by America's popular culture. This culture reflects the innovation that is the hallmark of American entrepreneurship and it has penetrated some of the world's most unlikely places.

Mickey Mouse, Michael Jordan and Madonna are universally identifiable. McDonald's Golden Arches have turned up in Paris, Rome, Nairobi, Tokyo, and Moscow. American films dominate cinemas and television screens. American football, baseball, and basketball are played or watched on every continent. Protest marchers in the streets of Belgrade wear caps bearing the name and emblem of the Pittsburgh Steelers. Levi's jeans are a hot fashion item and—much to the mystification of my generation—American popular music is heard, enjoyed and imitated.

Time to Use Our Economic Power to Achieve Security

But when all is said and done, America's greatest influence is economic. It possesses power which can win the support of friends and, at the very least, gain the undivided attention of enemies. Unlike the weapons of the military, devices that produce only death and destruction, economic power has the ability to enhance life and foster progress. By shifting the focus of international rivalry from armed confrontation to economic competition, the United States can help create a world in which every nation stands to prosper.

The U.S. has been magnificently successful in exporting both its products and its ideas. It has played a key role in creating a world in which trade is essential for survival. Yet, it has not fully understood the urgency of utilizing trade in a comprehensive effort to achieve international security. It has not exerted its leadership by shifting its focus from a defense based on military power to a defense that utilizes the power of the American economy.

By emphasizing economic rather than military power, the United States can enhance its ideological initiative. By speaking up for the powerless who are victims or potential victims of the machines of aggression, the United States can reassert the idealism that long was an admired foundation of American policy.

Innovation in the Cause of Peace

If the U.S. can succeed in building the world's most powerful economy, in exporting its ideas and dominating world culture, we can be equally successful in promoting the necessity of enforceable international law. With our enormous influence on the world's imagination, we can gain support for a civilized system of defense. We can make the concept of living without weapons of mass murder, of relying on economic power rather than military force, as popular around the world as Coca-Cola and other icons of American dominance.

The nation that takes pride in professing to be the champion of freedom should make clear its unshakable commitment to the Fourth Freedom. But the time for this bold humanitarian action is limited. The window of opportunity will not stay open forever. Each day wasted on trying to fine tune the disproven policies of the past moves the world another step closer to intended or accidental disaster.

It is ironic that the nation that delights in innovation has been far from innovative in its quest for lasting peace. The nation that developed incredible consistency in its hamburgers and french fries has been inconsistent in the development of policies that will end the threat of global disaster. The nation that leads in per capita college attendance, in the number of Nobel laureates and in opening its doors to the world's oppressed, has failed to lead in finding a way of protecting the people of all nations from the greatest threat to their existence.

The ability of the United States to exert a positive influence on international affairs has been proven again and again in recent years. The growing movement toward free trade and commercial liberalization owes much to American support. The extension for an indefinite period of the Nuclear Nonproliferation Treaty, the Dayton agreement to halt the war in Bosnia and other important initiatives could not have come to fruition without U.S. leadership.

America Is Admired around the World

A lifetime of experience has taught me that many nations look to America for direction and approval. There is a huge worldwide reservoir of admiration for the United States and what it stands for. Of course, the admirers get far less attention than the politicians who hunt for headlines by denouncing the U.S., the demonstrators who burn our flag, or the politicized mobs who shout "Yankee go home" or "Death to the Great

Satan." But from talking with business people and everyday citizens in countries around the globe, I can tell you America's admirers far outnumber its detractors.

Through the years, I have witnessed countless examples of the support that exists for America and its initiatives. Perhaps the most memorable incident occurred in 1960 when my wife and I spent a week vacationing at Bergenstock, high above Lake Lucerne in Switzerland. Most of the resort's guests were French, German or Italian and, on one strikingly beautiful night, nearly all of us were out dancing under the stars. All at once, the music stopped. High above us, we could see a bright object moving toward us across the heavens. It was going to pass directly over our heads and everyone seemed to know that it was Echo, the reflecting satellite that the United States had put into orbit. Where only minutes before the night was brightened by music, dancing and conversation, there now was silence. Then as Echo streaked over us, there was a spontaneous salute. Those who had been sitting at tables rose as one to join the dancers, raising their glasses in a toast we could understand: "Long live the United States of America!" Never have I been more proud to be an American.

The Western Europeans we were with that night knew the Soviet Union had launched Sputnik, the first object to achieve earth orbit. But they were cheering for the United States to take the lead in the race for space. They were applauding a symbol of our national effort, and the applause grew louder in 1969 when we reasserted our leadership in space exploration by a lunar landing. I am convinced the world's applause is as real today as it was more than three decades ago. I have heard it in the words and actions of individuals from many countries and through a range of business and social relationships.

I also have heard criticism, especially from our European friends. They understand that Americans are deeply imprinted with the European cultural tradition. The United States is Europe's child and, like all parents, Europeans sometimes are quick to criticize. They expect their child to fulfill many of their hopes. They believe America is destined to excel, to lead the world into a new age of achievement. If Americans prudently utilize their enormous economic power, if they strive for conciliation and work in cooperation with all nations who share the dream of peace and justice, freedom and opportunity, American leadership will be increasingly accepted everywhere.

Time to Renew Our Commitment to a Lawful World

The greatest barrier to this leadership is self-imposed. We are reluctant to exercise our might even if it is in our own self-interest. We are the world's only superpower but we do not like to be seen as forcing our beliefs and ideas on other nations. We sometimes are willing to nag or cajole but we rarely seem to understand all the other tools that are available to a leader. We have not quite decided how we should act and what we should do. And our inaction—perhaps paralysis is a better word—is eroding our ability to eliminate the greatest threat to our future.

Further delay is intolerable. The United States must act now to assume forceful leadership in a global effort to eliminate catastrophic weapons and acts of aggression. If the United States takes the initiative, it will be preserving not only the earth and its people but its own special heritage. It will be making sure that the precious gift of freedom will be handed down to our children and kept available to the children of all nations for all time.

If America's everyday individuals demand it, our country will renew its commitment to the values that contributed to its greatness. If everyday individuals step forward and become personally involved, the United States once again will rededicate itself to the principles of freedom, justice and opportunity. It will adopt a foreign policy that reflects its ideals, a foreign policy that will play an essential role in building a system of enforceable law that will bring to all nations the lasting security that ought to be the birthright of every member of the human race.

CHAPTER FIVE

Needed: A Foreign Policy Based on Principle

We often give our enemies the means for our own destruction.

—Aesop

Given America's abundance of economic and military power and the attractiveness of its traditions of liberty, democracy and opportunity, we ought to be achieving an unbroken string of foreign policy triumphs.

After all, we have just about everything the rest of the world wants. Why aren't we smart enough to use what we have to get what we want? Why can't we learn to use our assets constructively? Why do we so often fall into the win-lose trap of military action? Why don't we develop a win-win strategy based on our ability to reward those who join us in seeking new achievements for civilized society?

Instead, our nation lurches from crisis to crisis. We act as though we don't know where we want to go or how we want to get there. One hand seems to be encouraging peace while the other sows the seeds of war.

Rather than base our foreign policy on moral principle and world law, which are reliable and enduring, our leaders seek direction from public opinion polls, which are unreliable and temporary. Ignoring moral principle and world law, our leaders tack to the shifting winds of public opinion, a surefire recipe for disaster. No wonder we lack a concerted, long-term foreign policy. No wonder we are short of understanding and vision. Instead of foreseeing tomorrow's challenges and planning to meet them, America devotes its national energies to cleaning up yesterday's mistakes. We rarely initiate, we often respond. The thinking of our foreign policy establishment almost always is narrow, outdated and oblivious to the constantly evolving realities of a changing world. We give priority to expediency rather than morality.

I concede that in a democratic society, the gauging of public opinion must play a role in the difficult task of building a consensus on foreign policy. It is not easy to create a policy that is coherent, forward-looking and acceptable to the public. But it is dangerous to be without one.

A Dangerous Reliance on Confrontation

The danger is compounded by our almost total reliance on military power to influence the course of world affairs. In a re-creation of discredited nineteenth century gunboat diplomacy, we routinely use the threat of military action in an attempt to control events to our advantage. Like school boys who quickly run out of words, lose their tempers and start punching, we reveal our lack of intelligence and communication skills every time we abandon negotiations and launch an attack.

As Eugene J. Carroll, retired admiral, deputy director of the Washington-based Center for Defense Information and internationally recognized authority on military affairs, has pointed out, "This confrontational approach to foreign relations is extremely negative because it is based on coercion rather than efforts to develop constructive approaches of mutual benefit. It also creates pressure to use military force when significant issues lead to public awareness of pending problems with another nation. All too often the United States finds that gunboat diplomacy puts us in a position where the use of force will not resolve a problem but we will look foolish or impotent if we fail to act after threatening to do so."

In our dealings with Iraq, for example, we've blustered and bombed for the better part of a decade. Yet, despite heroic efforts by our armed forces and the expenditure of hundreds of millions of dollars, a dictator remained in control, the Iraqi people continued to suffer, and the security of the region was increasingly jeopardized. Instead of reaching out to the Iraqis, instead of doing our best to convince them that by over-throwing Saddam Hussein they can rightfully hope for a future of free-dom, opportunity, and national pride, we relied on confrontation backed by military might. We stepped into another foreign policy quagmire and the results were both predictable and humiliating. Worst of all, Wash-ington has given us no indication that it has learned anything from this or any other recent disaster in the international arena.

On the Korean Peninsula, to cite another example, an uneasy armistice has been in place since 1953. A demilitarized zone has separated the troops of the United States and its South Korean allies from a North Ko-rean army that is within artillery range of Seoul. The potential for re-newed, devastating conflict is great. Yet, our policy through the years has revealed no sense of urgency. Intoxicated by the knowledge of our mili-tary superiority, our policymakers veer from threats and counterthreats to embargoes of weapons and trade, to occasional gestures of humani-tarian aid and, finally, to what has been described as "benign neglect." Meanwhile, North Korea's leaders persisted in their pursuit of weapons of mass destruction and the long-range missiles required to deliver them. In this pursuit, North Korea appears to be following the example of the United States. It persists in the mistaken and discredited belief that the best way to achieve a foreign objective is through confrontation.

Why can't our foreign policy establishment understand that military power is a dead duck? Why can't our policymakers get it through their heads that the world has changed dramatically and the strategies of the past cannot master the realities of the present or the uncertainties of the future? Why can't we have a State Department staffed by people who are wise enough to figure out effective, reliable and nonviolent approaches to foreign policy problems? Why are we consistently inconsistent in our relationships with other nations?

Inconsistent Nuclear Policies

Look at the inconsistency of our policies relating to nuclear weapons, the single most important and dangerous problem facing not just the United States but all of global society. In 1995, we insisted on the per-manent extension of the Non-Proliferation Treaty. To obtain the agreement of nonnuclear nations, we joined the other four admitted nuclear powers in a joint statement committing to "The determined pursuit by the nuclear weapons states of systematic and progressive efforts to reduce nuclear weapons globally, with the ultimate goal of eliminating those weapons. . . ."

Two years later, President Clinton flatly renounced any intention to honor that commitment. In *Presidential Decision Directive Number 60*, he approved a policy which declared that nuclear weapons would indefinitely remain the cornerstone of U.S. security. Also included in the directive were other policies directly contrary to the nonproliferation goals that we claimed to support. For example, the directive affirmed the right to make first use of nuclear weapons, even against nonnuclear nations. It also called for maintaining a substantial nuclear force on hair-trigger alert status and for continued targeting of sites in both China and Russia.

While we advocated international support of the indefinite extension of the Nuclear Non-Proliferation Treaty, we continued to invest more than $30 billion each year in preserving and enhancing our capabilities for waging nuclear war. We were signaling to the world community that, despite the position we took in 1995, we continue to be addicted to nuclear weapons. We were indicating our lack of commitment to the underlying objectives of the treaty and giving nonnuclear nations an excuse to acquire or develop nuclear weapons of their own.

Dragging Our Feet on International Agreement

Our confrontational tendencies also are evident when we consider our unwillingness to join in cooperative international initiatives. In 1958, we provided strong leadership in the effort to create the United Nations Convention on the Law of the Sea. After 24 years of negotiation, in 1982 the convention was submitted to the world's nations for ratification. Its language met every U.S. objection except those concerned with seabed mining. That was enough to cause the U.S. to lead other industrialized nations in refusing to ratify the agreement.

In 1990, negotiations were resumed, the seabed mining issue was resolved and in July 1994, most industrialized nations, including the

United States, agreed to the convention. But even though the convention came into force on November 16, 1994, it did so without U.S. accession. In fact, it has yet to be ratified by the U.S. Senate.

As a result, our country has cut itself off from the development of a body of international law which covers 70 percent of the earth's surface and protects navigation, fisheries, the oceanic environment, and the wealth of the seabed. By going it alone, we are ignoring the contributions American leadership made to the shaping of the convention. We are rejecting another opportunity to demonstrate our belief in the necessity of world law and our understanding that under the rule of law all nations, including the most powerful, are equal.

There are other examples of America's willingness to choose confrontation over cooperation in its dealings with other nations. In 1998, we resisted broad international support for a permanent independent court empowered to try those accused of war crimes and other crimes against humanity, including genocide. We said we endorsed the idea of an international criminal court but we wanted it under the control of the United Nations Security Council where our veto would prevent the court from taking any action we deemed to be opposed to our interests. In the end, even our closest allies abandoned us and they were included among the 120 nations that voted against our position. Voting with us were just six other nations, including such exemplars of international lawlessness as Iraq, Libya, and Yemen.

Because the U.S. chooses confrontation over cooperation, we have delayed ratification of other important international agreements including the Comprehensive Nuclear Test Ban Treaty, the Convention on the Rights of the Child, and the Ottawa Anti-Personnel Land Mine Treaty. The Nuclear Test Ban Treaty was stalled in the U.S. Senate where Senator Jesse Helms, R-North Carolina, chairman of the Foreign Relations Committee, for a long time refused to schedule the hearings that would clear the way for a vote. The Convention on the Rights of the Child has been signed by 191 nations. The only nonsignatories are the United States and Somalia and, in the U.S., the convention has received minimal public or congressional scrutiny. The Ottawa treaty outlawing antipersonnel land mines has been signed by 120 nations while we stand in opposition with such nations as China, Iraq, Iran, Syria, Congo, and Cuba.

A Deep-seated Distrust of Others

In the case of the international Chemical Weapons Convention, which bans the manufacture, possession or use of chemical weapons, we signed on. This was a logical step in view of the fact that we are committed under our own law to eliminate our chemical weapons by 2004. But while the administration accepted the convention and the Senate ratified it, Congress has refused to appropriate the funds needed to implement the inspections required to verify compliance.

The refusal reflects a deep-seated distrust of the motives and intentions of other nations. Because of our enormous power, our leaders too often seem to believe that our standards should be world standards and that we alone have the right to impose these standards in any place and at any time. If there is any possibility that a global agreement will limit our freedom to act in what we perceive to be our own interests, we will reject the agreement or, if it survives our opposition, simply ignore its provisions. As Admiral Carroll reminds us, "The spirit of the world's remaining superpower seems to be, as President George Bush put it so eloquently, 'We call the shots.'"

Dominance Based on Confrontation Always Fails

In many ways, President Bush was correct. Yet, history teaches that not one of the great empires of the past was able to secure permanent dominance through confrontation backed by military force. The empires of Egypt, Assyria, Persia, Macedonia, Rome, Byzantium, the Ottoman Turks, the British, the Soviet Union and others flourished and then faded, leaving their mark on the future but failing to extend their hegemony beyond a limited number of years. The record demonstrates two truths: 1) Domination based on military power always fails because the people of the dominating nation sooner or later will refuse to make the necessary sacrifice of lives and money; 2) Those dominated sooner or later will rise up to overthrow the dominator.

In the absence of a credible military threat, Americans will not forever willingly pay the cost in blood and treasure of serving as the world's policeman. Year after year, we have maintained an overseas army of more than 200,000, put the lives of thousands of service men and women at risk and spend more than $280 billion in our attempt to guard every corner of the world. If the demands of the Pentagon are met, we could be spending as much as $350 billion a year in the new century, more on average than we spent confronting the Soviet Union during the 40 years of the Cold War.

As Americans tire of the policeman role their nation has assumed, the people of other nations will tire of America's military presence. When the Soviet Union had the armed might to threaten the territorial integrity of nations in Europe, Asia, and other parts of the world, the countervailing armed might of the United States was welcome. Now that the Soviet threat has vanished, we must expect that, sooner or later, the welcome mat will be rolled up and put back in the closet.

Other nations, understandably resentful of our dominance and our confrontational foreign policy, will not forever tolerate our presence. When these nations face up to the fact that American troops are poised to meet a nonexistent threat, they will not encourage our global military deployment. When other nations fully realize that our armed forces are instruments of a foreign policy that serves as an obstacle to international cooperation, they will act in their own best interest. They will say farewell to the self-appointed policeman and get on with the business of creating a world under law. If the people of the Philippines can throw us out after ninety years, what reason do we have to believe that others will not follow suit?

The Problem of Inconsistency

Besides, as with our foreign policy in general, there is little consistency in the way we carry out our policeman's role. For example, we repeatedly have declared our readiness to commit our service men and women to keeping the peace and preventing genocide in the former Yugoslavia. We do not make the same commitment in equatorial Africa, Tibet, Sudan, Sri Lanka or other focal points of violence and unrest. So we police the world on a selective basis, following the lead of the television cameras or bowing to the demands of voting blocks within our own country. If CNN isn't providing nightly pictorial coverage or if there is little chance to gain votes or contributions from Americans with overseas ties, the possibility of action by the United States drops to near zero.

Even when we do act, we often follow a misguided strategy that has been described as "muscular mediation." Instead of attempting to settle a dispute through negotiation that leads to compromise, we propose our own solution. Then we threaten to use our power against the side that rejects our proposal. We roam the world, scolding those who fail to do what we tell them to do and ready to begin bombing the nations that fail to meet the standards we set for them. We have assumed the role of global nanny, claiming that we know what is best for others and threatening to spank those who decline to obey our orders.

But in case after case around the world, our military leverage is weak or nonexistent. The threat of bombing is not likely to inspire the cooperation of a poor country with an undeveloped infrastructure nor will it generate fear among guerrilla fighters operating in jungle or mountainous terrain. Of course, we might be able to force an agreement by playing a trump card, the threat to deploy American ground troops. But if there is substantial risk that these troops would suffer casualties, the threat is not credible. No one with even a rudimentary understanding of American politics believes U.S. ground troops are likely to be dispatched to a place of danger. No American administration that is even remotely attuned to domestic public opinion will commit ground forces until the shooting has stopped and a cease-fire is in place. In the real world of violence spawned by ethnic and religious differences or by the actions of evil national leaders, muscular mediation is severely limited. It is nothing more than the old strategy of confrontation disguised with a trendy new label. And no matter what you call it, confrontation is a poor substitute for cooperation.

Time for Constructive Leadership

Clearly, it is time to get over our fear of other nations and provide the constructive leadership that will move the world toward the Fourth Freedom. We must join with our neighbors in a wide range of activities that can lead to a lawful world. We can begin by signing on to the Convention on the Law of the Sea. We can take steps toward worldwide nuclear disarmament, accept the rule of law by our endorsement of the jurisdiction of the International Court of Justice and the International Criminal Court and join with other nations in additional agreements that will contribute to reliable international security.

If we persist in the belief that we alone are authorized to proclaim and enforce our standards and judgments, we are doomed to isolation in a world increasingly ready to adopt global norms. Today we may be willing and able to carry out our policeman/nanny role. But tomorrow, or the day after tomorrow, it no longer will be affordable or possible for us to stand alone as the self-annointed rule maker and regulator of international relations.

Our Greatest Assets: Economic Strength and Democratic Ideals

Somehow or other our government must regain sight of the fact that our most important assets are not our troops and weapons but the strength of our economy and the power of our democratic ideals. These assets won our Cold War victory. Unfortunately, news of the victory did not seem to filter into our White House or State Department. Instead of using our success as a bridge into a new era of foreign and defense policies based on cooperation and principle, we held on to the beliefs of the past. We kept repeating the failed actions of bygone days. Instead of getting a firm grip on reality, we reasserted policies that reflected obsolete and disproven theories of international relations and national defense. Worst of all, we failed to confront the nuclear problem. We did not immediately take advantage of an unprecedented opportunity to at least make an attempt to put the nuclear genie back in the bottle. We continued to rely on nuclear deterrence to achieve our foreign policy goals.

The consequences of our failure to create a viable system for dealing with friends and enemies is apparent to all who will take the time to examine the record. Our unbending Cold War mentality may have been useful in its day but now it is strengthening the hand of those who oppose us and who reject our ideals. Our do-as-I-say-not-what-I-do stance undermines America's leadership and provides people around the world with a reason to doubt our sincerity and question our motives.

Power Now Resides with the People

With the virus of the Cold War continuing to infect our body politic, we seem unable to concentrate on building rapport with the people of all nations. Instead, we continue to emphasize diplomatic practices and policies that are as archaic as the top hats that once crowned the heads of ambassadors. Rather than treat the people of all nations as friends or potential friends, we stigmatize some nations as "rogues" and do little or nothing to end the rule of leaders who foment hatred and lawlessness. We don't seem to understand that, in the final analysis, there are no rogue nations. There are only rogue rulers and their authority is temporary because, in today's world, the ultimate power resides with the people.

The idea that authority comes from the people is a primary source of America's greatness. It makes government the servant, not the master. It assures national strength by empowering, indeed, demanding, that every citizen make a contribution to the common good. Our belief that authority flows upward from us, the grassroots citizenry, to those who represent us is powerful. It has played a key role in making America the wonder and the envy of the world.

The democratic ideal must be the foundation for all of America's national policies, including foreign policy. Our strategies and actions in the international arena must be thoroughly and publicly discussed by our elected leaders. Foreign policy decisions that could lead to armed conflict must be presented to Congress for ratification or rejection. The citizens of our nation, or any other nation, must not be plunged into war without open discussion of the objectives and risks. The sovereignty of the people must be confirmed whenever the nation confronts the life and death issues of military involvement.

Time to Stand Up for What Is Right

But there is a catch. For the people to constructively exercise their power, they must be united in their commitment to basic morality. If it is true, and I believe it is, that we live in a moral world that is part of a moral universe governed by laws that are immutable and beyond comprehension, we cannot be satisfied with a foreign policy that is divorced from morality. We cannot justify foreign policy actions and strategies that depend on confrontation and coercion. We must renounce a foreign policy that ignores the moral foundations of American society.

To put it in plain words, our present foreign policy is immoral. Only by abandoning it, by standing up for what is right and rejecting what is wrong, will we be able to treat the people of all nations with friendship, fairness and justice. Then we will be able to assure them that we will never use military force, except in self-defense or with the endorsement of the United Nations Security Council. And the people of other nations will believe that we are telling the truth.

To be the leader of the global society, the United States must put itself under the rule of law. We cannot have two moral standards, one for our own country and the other for the rest of the world.

Given the fact that today's technology has created a threat to humanity's future that is greater than any in the past, can we doubt the necessity of a lawful world? Can we not see that our survival depends on our ability to achieve an ever higher state of morality? Can we not understand that we have an obligation to take a moral stance that encompasses not just our own narrow self-interest, but the interests of the total world community?

We must remember that our ideas and beliefs, not our material or military achievements, are the substance of which civilizations are made. Our ideas and beliefs are the glory of all Americans. They are the things for which we shall be remembered.

CHAPTER SIX

A Time of Unprecedented Peril

*If we fail to seize the moment, history will never forgive us—
if there is a history.*

—Thomas A. Watson

Despite the fact that history is frequently ignored, it remains an instructor of incomparable reliability. It can help explain how we got where we are and, if we can overcome the natural temptation to deny reality, it also can serve as a trustworthy guide to where we want to be. Where we are, of course, is under the tyranny of weapons of mass destruction and it is ironic—and well worth remembering—that this tyranny has its origin in fear of a tyrant.

How the Bomb Came to Be

The World War II leaders of the United States and Great Britain knew that development of an "atom bomb" was theoretically possible. They were afraid Hitler's Germany might win the race to build one and they were certain Hitler would not hesitate to use it to destroy London and, sooner or later, other population centers in Europe and America. In response to this possibility, allied leaders mobilized the scientific community in an all-out effort to beat Germany to the prize, a weapon with unprecedented capacity for destruction.

Minimal consideration was given to the morality of nuclear warfare or the long-range strategic, environmental and humanitarian consequences of introducing a weapon of such great and little-understood power. The bomb seems to have been viewed as merely another step in the deadly progression from club to crossbow to gunpowder and beyond. President Harry S Truman, the man who ordered the bomb's first use against an enemy, wrote in his *Memoirs* (Doubleday & Company, Garden City, New York, 1955), "I regarded the bomb as a military weapon and never had any doubt that it should be used."

I well remember that many Americans cheered when Hiroshima and Nagasaki were incinerated. They believed that the earthshaking explosions saved American lives by shortening the war with Japan. Many also were convinced that the bomb was a technological triumph, a stunning confirmation of American might and invulnerability, an example of the dominance that publisher Henry Luce had in mind when he characterized the twentieth century as "the American century." There was no need to worry about the future. The secret of the bomb was in U.S. hands and why should anyone in the world be afraid of a country that was, at least in the view of Americans, so benign, so lacking in aggressive intentions and territorial ambitions?

Beginning the Nuclear Arms Race

What was largely overlooked by Americans was how other nations perceived the bomb. Some saw it as a new destabilizing element in the equation of international relations. Others resented this additional demonstration of American power. They worried about the possibility that it could be used by the U.S. to subjugate other nations for political, economic or ideological reasons.

Still others felt possession of nuclear weapons should become a pressing national goal because, if you had a bomb or two, perhaps you could settle the score by achieving some ancient ambitions or avenging some ancient wrongs. At the very least, if you had nuclear capabilities, no enemy would think of launching an attack. If an enemy somehow managed to match your nuclear arsenal, you simply could up the ante by adding more and more nuclear firepower.

Driven by fear or national pride, a number of nations pressed for membership in the nuclear club. During the post-Hiroshima years, as many as twenty-five of them took concrete steps to build a nuclear device. Some found the challenge too difficult, expensive or counterproductive and dropped out of the nuclear arms race. Others continue to this day.

Buying the Tools of Annihilation

Since 1945, an estimated $8 trillion ($8,000,000,000,000) has been spent on nuclear weapons by the nations of the world. According to the Brookings Institution, $5.5 trillion was spent by the United States alone in designing, producing and deploying nuclear weapons. By any standard, $5.5 trillion is a staggering amount, especially when you consider that the expenditures did not end with the Cold War. They continue to be made and the total continues to increase.

While the pursuit of nuclear goals absorbed the attention of the leadership of some nations, others were spending increasing shares of their economic resources on more conventional weapons. In some developing countries, military expenditures are the largest items in the national budget. Although overall military spending has declined over the past few years, world military expenditures in 1995 still amounted to more than $1.4 million every minute, according to *World Military and Social Expenditures 1996* by Ruth Leger Sivard (World Priorities, Inc., Washington, D.C.). If you include money spent on covert military activities, arming, training and maintaining paramilitary forces, the wages of workers building military goods and the construction and operation of facilities that produce materials that can be used either for peaceful purposes— generating power, for example—or for nuclear weapons, total military spending is beyond imagination or comprehension.

In the Soviet Union alone, some authorities believe as much as 25 to 30 percent of the gross national product (GNP) was committed to national defense each year from 1945 until the late 1980s. For the United States with its much larger economy, defense spending ranged from as high as 9 percent of GNP in the mid-1950s to a low of 4.7 percent in the late 1970s. In the 1980s, expenditures climbed above the 5 percent level and, since the end of the Soviet Union, they for the most part have been on the decline.

Even Smaller Nations Are in the Race

In some smaller nations, despite recent evidence of some easing of international tensions, military expenditures have continued to increase. Most of these nations lack the industrial base to produce their own modern weapons so they turn to outside suppliers. According to a study by Congressional Research Service for the eight-year period from 1988 to 1995, the United States sold $134.9 billion worth of weapons, Russia $73.6 billion, Great Britain $40.3 billion, France $32.5 billion, Germany $18.6 billion, China, $10 billion, Italy $4.3 billion and all other nations $41.7 billion.

For developing nations, expenditures of such size could only be accommodated through reduced investments in infrastructure, education and other programs that could have increased the rate of economic growth. For the U.S., respected economists believe military spending has had an overall negative impact on the national economy. It has consumed intellectual and material resources that could have been channeled into the development of new products for the world market. Because military expenditures are directed by a centralized authority and heavily influenced by the pressure exerted by Congress, the arms industry has been largely isolated from the competitive pressures that contribute to efficiency.

In all of its activities, including its sales to other countries, America's arms industry is heavily subsidized by U.S. taxpayers, making any profits questionable at best. Our government provides generous loan subsidies for the purchase of American-made weapons. Arms manufacturers increasingly offer coproduction and offset purchase arrangements that transfer jobs and production capacity abroad. In the U.S., 60 percent of government-funded research is military-oriented compared to 20 percent for countries of the European Union. These ratios raise questions of priorities. For example, what medical breakthroughs could have been made if more of the government's research dollars had been committed to the National Institute for Health? Instead, we spend great piles of money developing weapons which we then put on the market for sale to other nations. This transfer of technology not only compromises our arms leadership but it sometimes jeopardizes our safety. Weapons we developed are turned against us, as in Somalia, Haiti, and Panama. The arms race, and the arms trade that supports it, has produced many problems and few benefits. It has undercut our future and it has decreased, not increased, the security of the United States and other nations. It has failed to provide the reliable, efficient defense that ought to be desired by every American.

A Changed, Not Diminished, Threat

In the case of nuclear weapons, the threat to society has changed, not diminished. In 1967, the U.S. had 32,500 nuclear warheads. Since then, the numbers have declined. But as stockpiles have shrunk in America and in the Soviet Union and its successors, uncertainty has grown. At the start of the 1990s, the U.S. and the Soviets were thought to have a total of some 50,000 nuclear warheads, half strategic and half tactical. (The strategic category includes warheads for intercontinental ballistic missiles, submarine-launched ballistic missiles and bombs and cruise missiles delivered by long-range aircraft. Many of these weapons carry multiple warheads. Tactical nuclear warheads are designed for regional hostilities or for battlefield operations.)

Thanks to the dissolution of the Soviet Union, the Strategic Arms Reduction Treaties (START I and II) plus other international and unilateral initiatives, the number of strategic warheads has been decreasing. This downward trend, a refreshing indication that sanity has not totally vanished from our planet, also is affecting tactical nuclear warheads. Thanks to the Bush-Gorbachev actions of 1991, most U.S. and Soviet tactical nuclear warheads have been placed in reduced readiness.

However, there are at present no realistic expectations that either strategic or tactical warheads will totally disappear in the near future. Both the U.S. and Russia presently plan on continuing to possess thousands of strategic nuclear warheads and comparable numbers of tactical warheads. While it is unlikely that either nation will need to manufacture additional nuclear explosive material, they do intend to continue their efforts to upgrade the effectiveness of their existing nuclear weaponry. They are redesigning the weapons in their stockpiles and making use of the nuclear materials recovered from warheads on the verge of obsolescence. They are proceeding with subcritical tests and computer simulations that allow the testing and refinement of weapons designs without actual nuclear explosions. So while the number of nuclear weapons has declined from the early years of the present decade, the nuclear threat has not disappeared. It is incomparably greater today than it was in 1945 when the Enola Gay delivered its deadly cargo over Hiroshima.

Risks of Denuclearization

The threat is greater for several reasons. To begin with, the elimination of existing warheads involves procedures that are neither simple nor safe. A warhead cannot be abandoned, buried, shipped to a junkyard or put up on concrete blocks in your backyard. It must be dismantled by competent technicians using proven, precise techniques. In this process, uranium and plutonium must be removed. Then these extremely valuable and potentially dangerous materials must be stored for unknown years in a highly secure facility, reused in a nuclear reactor or, and here is the problem, recycled into other nuclear weapons. To prevent the metamorphosis of an obsolete weapon into an up-to-date one, to keep thousands of identified nuclear weapons from becoming tens of thousands of unidentified threats to humanity, the most rigorous verification process must be in place.

Every step of the dismantling procedure must be monitored by independent inspectors and every particle of nuclear fuel must be accounted for on a permanent basis. Today's technology for verifying and monitoring denuclearization provides a greater level of safety than ever before. In addition, progress has been achieved through U.S.-Russian arms reduction agreements which succeeded in including extensive arrangements for bilateral on-site inspections. The Nunn–Lugar Cooperative Threat Reduction program has given valuable assistance to Russia for the dismantlement and secure storage of decommissioned nuclear weapons. But despite these thoughtfully developed efforts, denuclearization still involves an element of risk. By tempting the nuclear want-to-be's, the dismantling of warheads could, at least temporarily, spread rather than contain the nuclear virus.

Nuclear Envy Persists

The desire to join the nuclear club has not been eliminated. In addition to the U.S. and Russia, France, Great Britain and China also are declared nuclear powers. China is thought to have perhaps 500 of these weapons while Britain and France each have something less than 500. India and Pakistan have forced their way into the nuclear club with their tests. Israel reportedly possesses as many as 100 to 200. Iraq, Iran and North Korea clearly have been devoting major shares of their resources to producing or acquiring their own nuclear arsenals. Argentina and Brazil dropped out of the nuclear race in 1991 when they agreed to a mutual program of inspections. South Africa earned the distinction of becoming the world's first postnuclear state when it agreed to dismantle the six nuclear weapons it says it produced prior to 1991.

Around the world, dictators, petty warlords, gangsters and extremists of every stripe long to come into possession of the ultimate weapon. To satisfy their ambitions, they will pay the price to acquire the bomb-making materials that are almost certain to become available as the largely bilateral nuclear disarmament process continues.

Still, we need to applaud the progress that has been made in denuclearization, especially since the end of the Cold War. Presidents Bush and Gorbachev achieved extraordinary results in reducing tactical nuclear weapons, concluding the Treaty on Conventional Forces in Europe and negotiating the START I and II Treaties. For present members of the nuclear club, the trend of expansion may have been reversed and there is increasing acceptance of the idea of total abolition of nuclear weapons. But there is little evidence that the world understands all that must be done to make abolition effective. Unless it is based on the bedrock of enforceable international law and not on the shaky ground of voluntary compliance, it will not work.

Danger Will Not Yield to Wishful Thinking

On the biological and chemical weapons front, there also has been progress. The United States is committed to destroying all its chemical weapons and, as noted earlier, has joined more than seventy other nations in ratifying the Chemical Weapons Convention. This treaty calls for the elimination of chemical weapons and provides for inspections to detect violations. Unfortunately, the U.S. has dragged its feet on inspections while Russia has delayed ratification and Libya, Iraq, Syria, and

North Korea, countries that have used chemical weapons or have tried to acquire the ability to produce them, have declined to participate. These are serious shortcomings. But even so, the Convention demonstrates how international law can be created through the treaty process and how worldwide public opinion favors significant reductions in weapons of mass destruction.

These trends are positive but I ask you to keep in mind an important fact: The world still lacks a comprehensive system of international security. The fear of a tyrant that ushered in the atomic age has largely been replaced by wishful thinking that tyrants somehow can be banned forever from the corridors of national power. Existing agreements, especially those made during the post–Cold War years, represent great strides toward world security but they do not deal with the possibility of irrational, destructive behavior in the White House or the Kremlin or in any national capital. They do not deal with the reality of political, ideological, ethnic or religious fanaticism. They cannot reassure those who worry that nuclear or other weapons of mass destruction will become increasingly available, that they will fall into the hands of renegade national leaders or terrorist groups.

Potential for Accidental Devastation

Achieved and proposed arms agreements also give insufficient attention to the possibility of technological or human failure. Policymakers often seem to assume that the weapons of annihilation and the people who control them are foolproof, that they will never malfunction or make mistakes—an assumption of perfection not likely to be endorsed by anyone who studies the record of accidents or near-accidents in the nuclear power industry and in the nuclear production facilities of both the U.S. and Russia. Indeed, safety problems already have shut down most U.S. warhead production sites.

The danger of an accidental nuclear exchange was made clear by an incident that occurred in January 1995. The trail of a rocket launched by Norwegian scientists was picked up by Russian radar. Because of bureaucratic fumbling, Russian radar crews had not been informed of the launching. Since the rocket was about the size of a submarine-based U.S.

Trident missile and since it seemed to be streaking out of the Norwegian Sea toward Russian airspace, technicians flashed an attack warning to Russia's military control center. The officers on duty relayed the warning to President Boris Yeltsin and top military commanders. Their electronics-packed briefcases were activated. Troops in charge of Russia's estimated 1,300 strategic missiles with 6,000-plus nuclear warheads were put on high alert. For perhaps 12 tension-filled minutes, Yeltsin and military authorities followed the progress of the rocket and pondered the scope of the counterstrike they could instantly order against the United States. Then just before the fateful buttons could be pushed, radar analysts determined the rocket was veering away from Russian territory and presented no threat. The alert was canceled, commanders breathed a very genuine sigh of relief and, once again, the world had dodged the bullet of nuclear disaster.

But suppose the radar evidence was inaccurate, inconclusive or misinterpreted. Suppose Yeltsin and the others were convinced the U.S. had ordered a sneak attack. Suppose they decided not to take a chance and to act before the supposed U.S. missile delivered a potentially crippling blow to Russia's military capabilities. The result would have been a nuclear exchange of such magnitude that it would have killed many millions, permanently scarred the face of our planet, and perhaps threatened life itself.

Dealing with a State of Denial

The 1995 incident—and other incidents that undoubtedly have occurred but which have not been reported—teaches an important lesson. Anyone who believes the world is safe from nuclear war is a victim of self-delusion. Anyone who objectively examines the present state of international security is bound to conclude that while conventional diplomacy has achieved many successes, it has been unable to build a solid foundation for the future of humanity. At best, the world's leaders have temporarily delayed the nuclear onslaught. At worst, they have created a distracting illusion that has kept humanity from concentrating on a lasting, inclusive solution to the threat posed by nuclear weapons.

This threat is not secret to anyone. A full-scale nuclear war would end life as we know it and almost no one believes a nuclear war could be anything less than full-scale for very long. As former senator John Culver once said, attempting to limit the use of nuclear weapons is like "limiting the mission of a match thrown into a keg of gunpowder." When people face up to the facts of nuclear peril, they are horrified—but not for long. The ordinary reaction is denial. Like those who choose to make their homes near the summit of an active volcano, they deny the existence of danger. They close their eyes to the destructive power of nuclear weapons, to say nothing of the threat posed by biological and chemical weapons.

Those who attempt to deny the danger sometimes excuse themselves by invoking the specious argument that "there's nothing I can do about it." They take refuge in a fatalism that is not far removed from moral paralysis. If the world is to survive, the paralysis must end. We must confront the threat posed by weapons of mass destruction. We must face up to the danger of nuclear weapons and their death-dealing biological and chemical cousins. We must commit ourselves to the realism of J. Robert Oppenheimer, one of the bomb's developers, when he described the 1945 testing of a bomb that, by today's standards, was puny. For him, the blast brought to mind a Hindu text from the *Bhagavadgita:* "The radiance of a thousand suns . . . I am become as death, the destroyer of worlds."

Time to Take Personal Responsibility

The chilling description underscores the choice we are being called on to make. We are being asked to exchange death for life, renounce the debilitating cult of fatalism, assume responsibility for our own future and accept the fact that survival in the nuclear age can only be assured through what Oppenheimer described as a "new type of international cooperation."

As M. Scott Peck, M.D., put it in his best-selling book *The Road Less Traveled* (Touchstone Books, Simon and Schuster, New York, New York 1978):

We cannot solve life's problems except by solving them. This statement may seem tautological or self-evident, yet it is seemingly beyond the comprehension of much of the human race. This is because we must accept responsibility for a problem before we can solve it. We cannot solve a problem by saying "It's not my problem." We cannot solve a problem by hoping that someone else will solve it for us. I can solve a problem only when I say "This is MY problem and it's up to me to solve it."

The threat of weapons of mass murder is our problem and it is growing, not receding, as the days and years roll by. To solve it, to reduce the dangers that face us, we must not be afraid to assume personal responsibility. We must become knowledgeable about the peril we face and courageous in exercising the new and expanding power of the everyday individual. Most of all, we must break the habits of the past as we pursue the goal of lasting security based on enforceable world law.

CHAPTER SEVEN

Confronting Global Evil

I believe that it is both wrong and foolhardy for any democratic state to consider international terrorism to be "someone else's" problem.

—Henry Jackson

When it comes to facing up to the dangers that now surround us, it's easy to give low priority to terrorism. We're comfortable pretending that terrorism is something that happens "over there." We remember the bombings of the World Trade Center and the Oklahoma City federal building but we are reluctant to accept the fact that these terrorist attacks well may have been the first strikes in a war that can shatter our complacency by penetrating the heart of an America that for decades seemed perfectly safe and secure.

If we are realistic in assessing what already has happened in our own country, we must come to the conclusion that a terrorist attack can happen any time and anywhere. It can touch us and our families in our churches, schools, offices, stadiums and shopping malls. It can take innocent lives, destroy property, disrupt transportation and communication and shatter the trust that binds together a democratic society. Our vulnerability is so evident that we willingly put up with inconveniences ranging from airport X-rays to the closing of Pennsylvania Avenue in front of the White House.

Yet, we also know that total security is beyond our grasp. A determined terrorist can penetrate the most elaborate defenses and, if the terrorist is armed with a stolen, homemade or blackmarket nuclear device, the devastation could be unimaginable. Once terrorists gain possession of weapons of mass destruction—a possibility that is rapidly increasing in our fragmented, post–Cold War world—their ability to disrupt our lives will be multiplied a thousandfold. Instead of striving to promote their cause through conventional bombings, assassinations or kidnappings, they will be able to blackmail governments by threatening to detonate a nuclear bomb, poison a municipal water supply or release nerve gas into a crowded arena unless their demands are met. Their "do it or else" message will be powerful because it will force authorities to decide if literally thousands of people will live or die.

Terrorism Is a Global Problem

In the past, terrorist threats and actions were frightening but they also were limited in impact. The Oklahoma City bombing sent a shockwave of sympathy, revulsion, anger and distress across the nation and around the world. But it did not bring the nation, or even Oklahoma City, to a halt. Will we be able to say the same thing when terrorists are capable of unleashing weapons with the power to destroy Washington or Los Angeles, Philadelphia or Jacksonville? Will our concern about terrorism increase in direct proportion to the number of fatalities, injuries and damage associated with an attack? When we fully realize that terrorists now are capable of the most fiendish and catastrophic acts of aggression, will we begin to comprehend that this is a global problem that must be dealt with on a global scale?

Difficulty of Dealing with Domestic Terrorism

Of course, there are homegrown terrorists, people who believe so fanatically in their cause that they will stop at nothing to carry it forward. They will murder, steal and burn to draw attention to themselves, advance their agenda and undermine the relationships on which all of us depend. They are as dangerous as they are incomprehensible. What drives them to turn the gift of freedom into a weapon that ultimately could bring freedom to an end?

Because of the rights we enjoy, the task of eliminating domestic terrorism is difficult. Police do not have, nor do we want them to have, unlimited investigative authority. We support the idea of giving law enforcement officers the tools they need to deal with the terrorism problem but we are understandably skeptical about allowing them unrestricted access to information about us and our families. We insist that law enforcement authorities walk the fine line that separates legitimate intelligence gathering from intrusion into our personal lives.

Risk Cannot Be Totally Eliminated

By defending our privacy, of course, we add to the problems faced by our antiterrorism efforts. But before we start apologizing for our commitment to our constitutional rights, we have to remember that even the most oppressive regimes have not been successful in eliminating domestic terrorism. During World War II, Nazi commanders dealt ruthlessly with the "terrorism" practiced by liberation movements in France, Belgium, the Netherlands, and other occupied countries but they could not be totally suppressed. In today's China, the threat of violence is taken very seriously by the ruling authorities, yet there continue to be reports of terrorist activities in support of the aspirations of ethnic minorities.

As long as fanaticism and paranoia exist, terrorism will be a fact of modern life and innocent civilians in America and other countries will be vulnerable to attack. But that does not mean we are powerless to minimize the danger. We have a right and a responsibility to protect ourselves and, while we know we will never be 100 percent successful, we can improve the present situation. The starting point is our willingness to accept the reality of danger. As with the continuing and expanding nuclear peril, we must not ignore the terrorist threat that faces us. Instead of trying to divorce ourselves from this perfectly justified fear, we ought to embrace it. It is a great source of motivation. It can drive us to constructive action. With fear—but not panic—in command, much can be done to improve our defenses against terrorist attack through technological advancements and a global assault on state-sponsored terrorism.

Improved Technology Can Help

Technology can help us do a better job of keeping track of explosives and armaments, including biological and chemical weapons. We can stop, or at least greatly reduce, the flow of weapons and other destructive materials into our country from abroad. We can improve security at airports, public facilities and other locations that are attractive targets for terrorist acts. Without violating the rights of individuals, we can enhance our ability to monitor the activities of potential terrorist groups. Because the terrorism problem has international dimensions, we must share our technological advances with other nations and, at the same time, take full advantage of their experience, knowledge and expertise. Through increased international cooperation, we will be enhancing our own security and contributing to the security of others.

But we must not stop with voluntary exchanges of information and equipment. We need to provide leadership. We must move with energy and conviction to mobilize the world community in a comprehensive effort to suppress terrorism wherever it occurs and whatever it is called.

Defining and Outlawing Terrorism

To begin with, we need to work with other nations in creating a definition of terrorism that can gain the acceptance of a clear majority of the nations and people of the world. This will not be easy. As the record of the United Nations General Assembly shows, definitions of terrorism have been debated, discussed and, sooner or later, abandoned. Much of the difficulty results from the suspicions of developing nations and minority groups. They tend to see the antiterrorism effort as a creation of large and powerful industrialized nations that want to suppress not just violence but revolutionary activity. They object to any definition of terrorism that does not provide exemptions for acts of violence committed in the name of self-determination, independence or anticolonialism.

While I understand the origins of this point of view, I cannot accept it. Murder is murder no matter what it is called. A child blown apart by a bomb thrown into a crowded market suffers and dies regardless of the announced motives of the bomber. A cause that needs to be advanced over the mangled bodies of innocent civilians is, at best, questionable. It merits the condemnation, not the tacit endorsement, of civilized society. Clearly, it is time for the world to create a definition of terrorism based on the accepted norms of civilization. Taking a life violates these norms. So does the capturing of hostages, the seizing or destruction of civilian aircraft and other violent activities designed to create the climate of fear that can paralyze a community or a country.

Enlisting the Aid of the Security Council

If the General Assembly cannot agree on a definition rooted in the accepted standards of civilized behavior, the Security Council has a responsibility to step in. Under the UN Charter, the Council is responsible for keeping the peace. Since terrorism is anything but peaceful and since it exacerbates the hostilities that lead to more widespread conflict, the Council needs to promulgate a straightforward definition of terrorism, declare terrorism to be a violation of international law and begin even-handed enforcement.

The Security Council already has shown some willingness to strike at terrorism. When Libya refused to extradite Libyan nationals suspected of perpetrating the heinous destruction of Pan Am Flight 103 over Lockerbie, Scotland, the Security Council imposed sanctions. When Sudan was implicated in the attempted assassination of Egyptian president Hosni Mubarak, the Council voted to impose partial sanctions in the form of a flight ban, although implementation of the resolution was delayed. While the Council's responses were less than vigorous, they demonstrated that international agreement on antiterrorism measures is well within the realm of possibility. Such examples, plus the recent history of cooperation within the Security Council, make me optimistic that it will outlaw all terrorism with minimum delay.

Global Law Is Essential

What is sorely needed, of course, is not ad hoc reaction to specific terrorist acts but international law prohibiting state sponsorship or encouragement of terrorism. The nation that breaks the law must be subject to penalties commensurate with the gravity of the violation. The nation that supplies weapons, provides training or offers a safe haven for fugitives, must be made to pay a price. It takes no great insight to understand that such nations are terrorist to the core. They flout international law, ignore the common standards of civilized society and violate the rights of their own citizens. Their governments rule by intimidation and they are consistent in seeking to impose their views on others. They have earned the condemnation of the global community and they must be subject to tough penalties that would effectively isolate them from the rest of the world.

Curbing the ambitions and the activities of terrorist states deserves a high priority. It will shrink the terrorist's source of support and reduce the threat of terrorism in every part of the globe. But attacking terrorism on a worldwide basis does not mean that the Security Council would be involved in the suppression of terrorism within the boundaries of a nation. It does mean that domestic terrorists would have more difficulty obtaining needed weapons, encouragement and assistance. Faced with the threat of rigorous sanctions imposed by the Security Council, a nation governed by reasonable people would quickly lose interest in an international terrorist agenda. If reasonable people are not in charge, if a nation persists in its commitment to terrorism, the Security Council must act decisively and promptly against those responsible for criminal behavior.

Terrorist States Must Pay a Price for Their Actions

Terrorism is a form of aggression and the terrorist is a potential weapon of mass destruction. So when Iran, Iraq, Libya, North Korea, Sudan, Syria, or any other nation sponsors terrorist groups that attack in order to destabilize their neighbors, they must be punished. If any nation offers sanctuary to terrorists, it must be subjected to severe penalties and these must be applied by all law-abiding nations. The world must not tolerate halfhearted, incomplete enforcement of the law. It must not permit a repetition of recent history when, for example, U.S. efforts to force Libya to give up terrorist suspects were frustrated by the desire of other nations to buy Libyan oil and supply Libya with manufactured goods, including equipment that could be used to produce poison gas.

What is called for is not ineffective unilateral action but a global effort to shut down the international networks that foster terrorists and their activities. If the Osama bin Ladens of the world can find no sanctuaries and if they no longer can obtain the documents needed to pass through international boundaries, the threat of terrorism will be diminished. If explosives and advanced weaponry become less and less available, the danger will lessen. While terrorists motivated by ethnic, religious or other forms of fanaticism will still exist in many parts of the world, they will have lost much of their ability to intimidate and assault the innocent and paralyze the institutions of civilized society.

The benefits are obvious. Businesses, financial institutions and other organizations will be able to invest in locations that once were considered unacceptably dangerous. Commerce will expand. Jobs will be created. Travel will increase. Men and women will be able to take advantage of expanding opportunities for themselves and their families.

Genocide Must End

While our concern with terrorism is both understandable and important, we must not forget that during the present century genocide has taken far more lives and inflicted much more suffering than all the terrorist acts combined. In Europe, Asia and Africa, millions were slaughtered because of their ethnic origins, religious beliefs or cultural traditions. Men and women were tortured, families butchered, children left to die of hunger or disease, possessions confiscated, homes and villages destroyed while most of the world community did its best to look in another direction, to see or hear no evil.

While people of goodwill acknowledged that genocide is perhaps the most despicable crime against humanity, the perpetrators rarely have been brought to justice. Leaders of supposedly civilized nations were too concerned about the international balance of power to risk doing anything about savagery in another country or on another continent. The arrest and prosecution of those who crush defenseless minorities is often discussed but rarely attempted. Only in recent years, with the war crimes tribunals for Yugoslavia and Rwanda, have efforts been made to identify and punish those who plan and carry out genocidal policies. Without an institutionalized and clearly understood system of international law and law enforcement, the world community can wash its hands of the victims' blood by claiming a lack of authority or jurisdiction.

In a lawful world, crimes against humanity will be defined, statutes will be in place and the enforcement mechanism will be ready. Genocide no longer will be ignored. Victims will have the law on their side and a criminal justice system ready to hear their cries for assistance. The leaders who order mass killings and the underlings who carry out immoral commands to murder men, women and children will be brought to justice and the cause of civilized behavior will take another step forward.

Benefits of a Nonviolent Solution

With genocide as with terrorism and every other international issue, a nonviolent approach to the problem will foster the evolution of a less violent world. Nations will begin to see the wisdom of reducing the size and rethinking the purpose of their armed forces. The emphasis will be on weapons that utilize computer, laser, optical, electronic and other advanced technology. Armies will be smaller and more mobile and, in keeping with the developing trend in human society, the initiative of the individual soldier will be more important than ever. The army of the future will be more attuned to a defensive strategy. It also will be better prepared to respond to the requests of the Security Council as it calls on national governments and regional military alliances to assist in the enforcement of international law.

NATO Expansion: A Step in the Wrong Direction

The military alliances—NATO is a good example—also will have to rethink their mission in a world committed to the rule of law. NATO was created to prevent the Soviet Union from overrunning Western Europe and to provide a reason for keeping U.S. forces on the scene. With the fall of the Soviet Union, the threat of invasion disappeared, but not the memory of past invasions. As a result, many Europeans find the continued presence of U.S. troops comforting. They also like the constant communication that has contributed to unprecedented European stability. They appreciate the unity that has made war among NATO partners almost unthinkable.

By most standards of measurement, NATO has been remarkably successful, a judgment underscored by the applications for membership submitted by Central and Eastern European nations that not long ago were part of the Soviet bloc, NATO's avowed enemy. Despite understandable objections by Russia, the expansion of NATO is an accomplished fact and, in my view, a serious mistake. Bigger is not necessarily better. More members do not necessarily make an organization stronger. Indeed, expanded membership increases the possibility of internal tensions. Does it make sense to suggest that we might go to war if Poland has a dispute with Hungary? Will not the military effectiveness of NATO diminish as it spreads its commitments and obligations over additional members? The major security issues in today's Europe do not involve invasion by some outside power. They are terrorism, civil wars, narcotics trafficking and the "loose nukes" threat created by the dissolution of the Soviet Union. NATO was not designed to deal with these issues. It is the wrong tool for today's security needs.

NATO expansion will increase the number of weapons in Europe and, as history teaches, the more weapons that are available, the more likely is the possibility that they will be used. Arms buildups do not bring peace. They contribute to an attitude of invincibility that encourages war.

NATO expansion also means increased costs, but the value of the benefits that will be derived from the cost increase is far from certain. Would not the billions of dollars that will be spent on NATO expansion produce more positive results if they were invested in helping Russia and its former allies improve their economies? Would not the time, energy and brainpower expended on expansion pay bigger dividends if they were used to weave Russia and its former allies into the fabric of the European economy?

Look to the Future, Not the Past

Through the Marshall Plan of post–World War II, we helped a defeated Germany get to its feet, strengthening the European economy and blocking the westward expansion of the Soviet empire. Policies with similar objectives helped revive a defeated Japan. Now the vanquished enemy is Russia and it, too, could be assisted by a resurrection of the Marshall Plan concept. We share space programs with the Russians. Why can we not also share some economic programs?

The expansion of NATO reflects a human tendency to preserve even obsolete institutions. The desire of NATO's three newest members— the Czech Republic, Hungary, and Poland—to become more closely connected with the industrialized West and the eagerness of American politicians to pander to the perceived interests of ethnic voting blocs were entirely predictable. Expansion also demonstrates the sad fact that bureaucracies never put themselves out of business and it reveals thinking that is woefully out of touch with the times. Instead of taking advantage of a growing international demand for the extension of the rule of law, the politicians and policy specialists promoting NATO expansion gave precedence to tinkering with an old-fashioned military alliance in the vain hope that it can survive the massive changes that are transforming the world. Those responsible for NATO expansion seem unaware of the trends that are shaping the days ahead. As we have been discovering in our search for the Fourth Freedom, democratic ideals are flourishing, military options are increasingly discredited and individuals are interacting on a global scale for education, information and understanding.

The rationale for a military alliance, even a NATO that includes Russia, should not be the same today as it was yesterday and it certainly will not be the same tomorrow as it is today. Before NATO was expanded, it should have been reevaluated. Its mission, organizational structure and operations need to be reconfigured to meet the requirements of a society that is moving away from violence and toward nonmilitary solutions to international problems.

A Healthy Conversion from Military to Civilian Production

The shift from military power to economic power for the enforcement of civilized conduct will not mean the extinction of the military. The United States and other nations will continue to need committed men and women to defend us from external enemies. But opportunities for careers in the military surely will decline and, just as surely, we will have to come to grips with the fact that the chief purpose of the military is national defense, not employment. It does not make economic or political sense to maintain a large standing army in order to provide more jobs. The best jobs are those that allow men and women to be productive members of society and the great majority of these are to be found in private industry.

During the 1990s, we have seen shrinkage in U.S. defense spending. At the same time, the civilian economy has been healthy with steady growth, low inflation and unemployment rates that are the envy of other industrialized democracies. From this experience, it is clear that defense shrinkage does not necessarily mean overall economic shrinkage. Indeed, I think it would be sensible to argue that cutbacks in defense spending will stimulate, not depress, the economy.

As the need for the defense industry's products declines, some companies will be able to modify production and adapt technologies to compete in civilian markets. Freed of the rigorous requirements of Defense Department procurement policies, some of these companies will be able to extend their records of successful operation. While their employment quite likely will decline from the arms industry's boom years, these companies will continue to be profitable and they are likely to stay in business for many years.

Some other arms producers will not survive the transition. After years of depending on government contracts, they will find themselves unable to adapt to the competitive environment of the civilian market economy. The result will be hardship for shareholders, employees and communities. To soften the blow, politicians will call for governmental assistance and a variety of federal, state and local agencies will implement programs designed to assist the conversion from military to civilian production and to provide retraining and other help for those who will find themselves unemployed. But the long-term solution to the problem created by cutbacks in defense spending is not government involvement. It is a buoyant, expanding economy.

Time and again, a strong economy has overcome the difficulties created by technological advancements and changing demands in the marketplace. When the transistor proved its superiority over the vacuum tube in radios, televisions and other electronic gear, a number of companies, including such giants as RCA, were unable to make the transition to transistor production. Plants were closed, jobs were terminated and, to those directly involved, the future looked bleak. But a new generation of companies, Texas Instruments and Intel, for example, soon appeared on the scene, leaping beyond transistors to electronic chips, stimulating the creation of entirely new categories of products and expanding employment opportunities in production, distribution and marketing all across the country.

Contributing to an Expanding Economy

With a strong economy, the shrinking of the defense industry will be viewed not so much as a threat, but as the opening of an expressway into the future. A strong economy will make it possible to convert to civilian use some of the sophisticated technology utilized in armaments. The know-how required to build today's advanced weapons systems well may find a place in building an array of useful civilian products that now exist only in the imagination. Many of the skills of defense industry workers will be sought after by companies eager to take advantage of the unique properties of composites and other materials originally developed for military purposes.

An expanding economy will increase the ability of the private and public sectors to invest in research specifically targeted to meet the needs of our civilian population. We will be able to increase our support of space exploration, earth sciences, oceanography and other programs that promise to increase our knowledge of the world in which we live and improve the lives of our children and grandchildren. Instead of living in fear of atomic energy, we will unlock more of its secrets and learn more about how it can be used to enhance rather than destroy life and the planet upon which life depends.

In the world of the Fourth Freedom, our fear of the atom, like our fear of terrorism, genocide, armed aggression and weapons of mass murder, no longer will distract us from our lives. We will have increased ability to pursue our interests and achieve our goals. In a lawful world, trade will expand and the economy will grow, not only in America, but on every continent and in every country with the courage to stand up for the values that civilized society transmits from generation to generation.

Our responsibility is to make sure our values are protected from the violence of lawlessness and from the reluctance or inability of our leaders to adapt to the new realities of society. By accepting the responsibility, we will not be guaranteeing paradise on earth. We will be making progress in our effort to discover a system that will reliably protect the world from evil.

CHAPTER EIGHT

Proclaiming the Primacy of Law

I wish to see the discovery of a plan that would induce and oblige nations to settle their disputes without cutting one another's throats.

—Benjamin Franklin

So far, our effort to discover a plan that will free the world from throat-cutting on a global scale has turned up some significant clues. We've come face to face with the incredible opportunities of the present moment, a time when dictatorships are giving way to democracy and the empowerment of the individual is transforming and renewing nearly all of our institutions. We've encountered the vital necessity of United States leadership and we've reviewed persuasive evidence of the obsolescence and inherent inadequacy of military power. At the same time, we've relearned a lesson that has been presenting itself to us for a lifetime: economic power is a dominant force in shaping and regulating human behavior.

We've also confronted some of the less comfortable aspects of the here and now. All of us are in the crosshairs of disaster. We are targets or potential targets of an array of weapons that have the power to destroy the human race, incinerate our planet and put an end to the future. Terrorists roam the world, threatening our lives and our peace of mind. The cloud of genocide darkens vast areas of the earth and innocent families continue to be slaughtered solely because of their racial, ethnic or religious identification.

As we explore the landscape of the here and now, we become aware of both the danger that surrounds us and the invitation that strengthens our hope. It is an invitation to mobilize our intellects and our energies in a bold campaign to break the bonds of fear through broad acceptance of the global rule of law.

Law: The Foundation of Global Security

Unless we accept the primacy of law, even the best intended efforts to achieve international security will fail. Without law, no social structure can survive. The lawless family, tribe, community or nation condemns itself to destruction. It inevitably will ruin itself and, very likely, many of those that come in contact with it. Lawlessness is a disease that must be suppressed or quarantined. If it is encouraged or even tolerated, it will produce deadly results.

While we may understand the essential role law plays in human relationships, we sometimes are reluctant to accept its practical application and its influence on the decisions of our daily lives. As individuals, we may find ourselves inclined to ignore a law that causes us inconvenience or costs us money. As a nation, we sometimes choose to flout laws that appear to interfere with our perceived national interests. Then we offer excuses for our bad behavior. We rationalize our lawbreaking actions and do our best to pretend that our crime was trivial and will have no lasting consequences.

But when it comes to the present international situation, nothing is trivial and the consequences of lawlessness could be annihilation. The weapons are ready and they can strike their targets in a matter of minutes. There is only one way we can protect ourselves and that is through global acceptance of laws prohibiting terrorism and armed aggression and banning the possession of any weapon of mass destruction.

A Declaration of International Will

These laws could take the form of treaties, conventions or enactments by the United Nations. They could be drafted from scratch or they could build on existing international law by closing loopholes and eliminating ambiguities. The important thing is not the law's pedigree or structure but its substance. Using language that is brief, pointed and understandable, it must provide a simple, direct and unmistakable reflection of the will of an overwhelming majority of the world's nations and people.

Given the preeminence of America's position in world affairs, it is reasonable to suggest that the initiative for antiaggression, antiweapons law come from the United States. But those responsible for the law's development must take care that it is not seen as a U.S. invention. It must not be looked on as a made-in-the-USA attempt to promote an American agenda. It must be perceived for what it really is: A straightforward, common sense law that promotes the agenda of every nation and every individual.

The U.S. declaration of support for the law should be the culmination of extended consultation with the leaders of other nations. In an informational, nonthreatening manner, the U.S. should describe its intentions and seek broad international support. By constantly and openly communicating its intentions, the United States will be helping shape global public opinion, paving the way for other governments to join in endorsing a civilized plan for dealing with the threats posed by aggression and weapons of mass destruction.

The United States and other nations initially endorsing the plan will encourage voluntary support. But they also must make it clear that nations accepting the primacy of law will be extended the privileges of trade and the benefits of economic cooperation. Nations that refuse to endorse the law or that violate the law's precepts will be subject to economic sanctions.

A Pragmatic Formula for Ratification

The antiaggression, antiweapons law will go into effect when it is ratified by two-thirds of the nations of the world, including those doing two-thirds or more of all trade in manufactured goods. The formula is based on the necessity of cooperative action. It requires the involvement of an unquestionable majority of the industrialized nations, the nations that produce much of the goods and services needed by the world, the nations that have the economic power to assure effective law enforcement.

Putting responsibility for the enactment of a world-changing law on the shoulders of the industrialized nations is not intended as an affront to those that are less developed. It is a recognition of reality. The developing nations do not have the power to destroy the world. It is the industrialized nations with their arms-building capabilities that have brought the world to the brink of the nuclear abyss. By pulling back, by renouncing aggression and eliminating weapons of mass destruction, they can make a profound contribution to world stability and prosperity. They can create conditions that will benefit the least developed as well as the most developed nations.

When I discuss the ratification formula with friends or associates, I often am surprised by their initial reaction. Americans in government, academia, law, business and many other walks of life, even those who are part of what is described as "the peace movement," express considerable skepticism. Some see all kinds of obstacles. Others say flatly that the formula will not work. When I ask them why they have a thumbs-down reaction to a formula based on the two-thirds principle so universally accepted by democratic society, I hear a variety of answers. But in the final analysis, all are based on fear. The naysayers are afraid people are not the same the world over. They are afraid the people of other nations do not want the same things we want for ourselves and our families.

A Universal Aspiration for Protection

My experience has taught me a different lesson. I believe people of varied national identities and cultural backgrounds are fundamentally the same. They need food, clothing and shelter. They want the opportunity to earn a living, utilize their talents and practice their religion. They also want to be free of the threat of devastating war. Their desires, shared by people around the globe, explain my faith in the eventual affirmation of a system of international law and its nonviolent enforcement.

Besides, I believe there is safety in numbers and wisdom in the thinking of ordinary men and women. Even under the rule of the most fearsome dictators, common sense does not totally leave common people. If two-thirds of the world's people approve the idea of an international law abolishing weapons of mass destruction and armed aggression, enforcement will not be a problem.

If the people of a nation want something strongly enough, their leaders sooner or later will have to grant it. President Dwight D. Eisenhower said that people will someday want peace so much that governments will have to get out of the way and let them have it. When the people and their leaders recognize that law has the potential to free the world from fear, the adoption formula will offer a common sense way to bring the potential to reality. By requiring international law to be adopted by two-thirds of all the world's nations, a strong and lasting base of support will be assured. A simple majority, one that can disappear with the defection of a few nations, is not enough for a law that is so important to all the world's people.

A Two-Thirds Majority Is Proven and Practical

A two-thirds majority possesses no magic. But it does have a long and honorable tradition in democratic society. It has been used around the world as a standard of decisive popular or parliamentary support in matters of great consequence. America's founding fathers included it in a Constitution that has endured for more than 200 years. It is the margin required for domestic ratification of international treaties. The formula has proven itself again and again. It is useful, workable, understandable and effective.

In the endorsement of global antiaggression, antiweapons law, the formula has both political and economic dimensions. To achieve strong political support, it requires the endorsement of two-thirds of all nations. To assure the powerful economic support that is necessary for law enforcement, it calls for endorsement by nations doing two-thirds of the world's trade in manufactured goods. In this way, the antiaggression, antiweapons law will enjoy the support of an unquestioned majority of nations and a preponderance of the world's manufacturing capacity. When the law goes into effect, I believe it will be backed by nations large and small, rich and poor.

Why Nations Will Ratify the Law

But another question persists: Why can we expect any nation to adopt a law or a body of laws that breaks so sharply with established, though obviously inadequate concepts of international security?

The answer for developing nations ought to be clear. They have much to gain from an enforceable law that will ban aggression and eliminate weapons of mass murder. These nations face serious problems of hunger, disease and illiteracy. Yet, many of them typically spend a disproportionate share of their financial resources on armaments. They need better seeds, more fertilizer and improved agricultural practices. They have shortages of schools and teachers, physicians and clinics. Yet, they continue to buy guns and tanks and military aircraft.

As President Eisenhower once declared,

> Every gun that is made, every warship launched, every rocket fired signifies, in the final sense, a theft from those who hunger and are not fed, those who are cold and not clothed. This world in arms is not spending money alone. It is spending the sweat of its laborers, the genius of its scientists, the hopes of its children. . . .

Yet, according to *World Military and Social Expenditures 1996*, developing nations spent $107 billion on their military in 1993 compared to $69 billion on health and $125 billion on education.

The same publication also provides a list comparing the cost of military protection to the cost of social protection, a list that illustrates what would be possible if priorities were changed and military expenditures were diverted to meet social needs. For example, a single *Abrams* M1 tank upgraded with improved armor and nuclear/biological/chemical protection carries a price tag of $5.8 million, enough money to provide 530,000 vials of insulin for diabetics in low-income countries. A *Tomahawk* cruise missile costs $2.35 million, an amount that would drill more than 1,600 wells equipped with hand pumps for families without local water resources. The cost of an *Aegis* guided missile destroyer, $969 million, would pay for an extra year of primary education for children in least developed countries.

One of the reasons these countries are impoverished is the lack of modern infrastructure. Without adequate roads, bridges, ports and pipelines, electrical generating and distribution capacity, and modern telecommunications systems, economic development cannot take place and, without economic development, families cannot find the employment they need to lift themselves out of poverty. Unfortunately, infrastructure development often is given a lower priority than the continual upgrading of a military force equipped with the best weapons money can buy. Too often, national leaders prefer to invest scarce resources in an army that may never be used rather than in an infrastructure that is sure to have lasting positive economic and social impact.

Since the end of the Cold War, weapons purchases by developing nations have declined. But existing stockpiles of weapons still far exceed those deemed essential by any rational assessment of need. Despite the fact that most recent wars have been civil rather than between sovereign states, many national leaders continue to find a bogeyman beyond their borders that can be used to justify the high cost of maintaining an army.

Economic Tools Will Encourage Ratification

When the debate over the antiaggression, antiweapons law begins, leaders of the governments of developing countries cannot be expected to leap to their feet in enthusiastic response. They do not think of themselves as facing the direct threat of nuclear attack and, with a few exceptions in the Middle East and the Far East, neither they nor their neighbors have the capacity to wage chemical or biological warfare. Their problems—exploding population and unemployment, for example—may appear to them to be more immediate and dangerous than the possibility of armed aggression or the existence of weapons of annihilation. Because the economies of these nations are in a primitive state of development, they cannot be expected to take the lead in promoting an international system of defense. A nation with a manufacturing sector that is nearly nonexistent and an economy that is so debt-burdened that its imports are drastically limited has little to fear from many forms of economic penalties.

The stick of sanctions would have little effect on such a nation. But the carrot of incentives is another story. Developing countries could be enthusiastic supporters of a world ruled by law if they understood its many benefits, if they realized the economic, technical and other advantages that would be integral parts of a law-based system of international security.

Sanctions Must Be Targeted and Humane

In the unlikely event that the imposition of sanctions becomes necessary during the law's ratification phase, they should be as humane as possible. They should target leaders, not everyday citizens. Given today's global electronic financial system, the possibilities of freezing the overseas assets of national leaders are improving. Travel bans are also a form of targeted pressure. Such measures can prevent leaders from traveling outside their country. It would be simple to inflict economic hardship on them by cutting off their sources of income from enterprises that have an international dimension.

Such targeted economic sanctions would, at the very least, get the attention of a country's leadership and, because targeted sanctions would have little effect on ordinary citizens, they would not provoke what has been called the "rally around the flag" effect. They also would not put great added strain on an already fragile economy and they would not punish citizens who had little or nothing to do with their government's refusal to ratify the antiaggression, antiweapons law.

If the imposition of sanctions becomes necessary to secure ratification of the law, they should not include the earth goods that are essential for human survival. Prohibiting trade in earth goods, especially agricultural products, would punish the innocent, increase tensions and threats of counteractions while having only a marginal effect on the near-term capacity of a country to wage aggressive war. For the same practical and humanitarian reasons, health care supplies, including medication and equipment, also would be exempt from any trade embargo.

In building a structure of law and law enforcement, the principal focus should be on the industrial products that are essential to the development and maintenance of an arsenal of nuclear, chemical and biological weapons. As I have said, in today's global economy, no nation can be completely self-sufficient in the products of manufacturing. Even the United States would experience hardship if manufactured products were withheld from it. For most other nations, including those with advanced economies, the withholding of these products would strike a devastating economic blow, make long-term aggressive behavior more difficult and provide a persuasive reason to ratify the law with minimum delay.

Alternative Routes to Ratification

The mechanics of the ratification process could involve several alternative courses of action. The most obvious would be introduction of a resolution of endorsement in the General Assembly of the United Nations. Delegates from all nations would be free to state their views in a central forum and the give-and-take of debate would be reported around the world by the mass media. The problem is that the General Assembly is largely an advisory body and, over the years, it has not distinguished itself as a forceful voice in world affairs. In the General Assembly, a one-nation-one-vote system is in effect and the smallest country's vote can offset the vote of the largest. If the General Assembly approves a resolution, it passes its action along as a recommendation to the Security Council. The Council, in turn, is free to approve or ignore whatever the General Assembly recommends.

For a resolution as important as the one mandating the global rule of law, the shortcomings of a General Assembly ratification process would have to be addressed. Approval of the resolution would have to become binding, not optional, and the votes of member nations would have to be weighted to take into consideration their involvement in international trade. If achieving these changes proves to be too cumbersome or difficult, the General Assembly could be bypassed, as it has been on many matters of grave importance for more than a half century. Then the resolution of endorsement could be presented directly to the governments of the nations of the world.

Direct, nation-by-nation presentation of the resolution would bring the issue of enforceable international security to the attention of citizens in the familiar setting of their own governmental procedures. The debate would be closer to home and more subject to the influence of national political considerations. In a democratic society, the vote by a parliament likely would reflect with considerable accuracy the views of the electorate on an issue of lasting, undeniable importance. On the negative side, the nation-by-nation presentation process might prolong discussion and delay urgently needed action.

Why Not a Single Question Assembly?

Perhaps the most reasonable approach to ratification is the creation of an assembly empowered to deal with a single question—the endorsement and implementation of the rule of law. Such a limited purpose assembly could be convened by the Security Council or by the United States and other nations acting in concert. The assembly would exemplify the democratic tradition by respecting the right of all people in all nations to be heard. It could convene in New York or Tokyo or, for that matter, in Santiago or Bombay. But it seems to me that it would be far more appropriate in this computerized age if official delegates gathered in cyberspace so their deliberations could circle the globe in a network of unity and hope. Ordinary citizens could plug into the proceedings, demonstrating their interest, increasing their understanding and providing their support. They could contribute to the success of a town meeting of the world, a town meeting that could shape the direction of civilization for decades to come.

Even if messages are transmitted with the speed of light, ratification will not be accomplished in a matter of days. No matter how the process is organized, it will be weeks or months before there is sufficient agreement to establish a world under law. After all, creating a workable system of law and law enforcement requires a new way of thinking about the problems we face and the opportunities we have been granted. It calls for accepting the economic realities of today's world and turning away from centuries of reliance on military force. Making this turn in the proper direction will be like maneuvering a supertanker. When the captain changes the position of the rudder, nothing seems to happen at first. Then slowly and carefully, the bow begins to swing around and the ship gradually steams ahead in a new direction.

Sharpening Definitions and Closing Loopholes

But while the world is turning toward law and its nonviolent enforcement, while the ratification process is in progress, peace does not need to be put on hold. Much can be accomplished while nations consider declaring their support for the law and joining the community of the law-abiding. During the ratification period, details of enforcement can be discussed and the machinery of enforcement can be made ready.

Before any antiaggression, antiweapons law is finally approved, the UN also should reexamine the definition of weapons of mass destruction that was included in its own resolution of 1948. This definition includes ". . . atomic explosive devices, radioactive material weapons, lethal chemical and biological weapons and any weapons developed in the future which have characteristics comparable in destructive effect to those weapons. . . ."

The definition is broad. But the world needs to be sure that it covers every possible instrument of mass terror, that it takes into consideration the technological advances made since 1948 and the breakthroughs that are likely to occur during the years ahead. Does it cover laser weaponry? Electromagnetic pulse devices? Information warfare designed to paralyze the computers on which industrialized society depends?

And what about the definition of aggression? Can the world agree on language that accurately differentiates between offensive and defensive conduct? Are there words that can unmistakably draw the line separating acceptable from unacceptable behavior? Can people of goodwill go beyond national, cultural, sectarian and semantic differences to decide the supposedly simple question of what is right and what is wrong?

As a result of many years of consideration, the United Nations already has agreed on a binding definition of aggression but, to achieve a consensus, a few escape hatches were left open. In my view, these can easily be closed by reasonable people who are sincere in their commitment to building a law-based world.

If the world's leaders understand that the rule of law enjoys strong public support, they will do what is right. With the promise of security so near at hand and with international attention so sharply focused on them, I am convinced they will overcome narrow national and political interests. By coming down on the side of principles that command respect for the law, they will assure their place in history. They will contribute to the continued uplifting of human society by moving the world a step closer to the Fourth Freedom.

CHAPTER NINE

Taking a Stand
for Nuclear Freedom

The way to win an atomic war is to make certain it never starts.

—Omar N. Bradley

If we want to make certain a nuclear war never starts, we can't stay on the sidelines. We can't sit passively waiting for the world to wake up to the necessity of enforceable international law. We know from the search we've been undertaking that the discovery and implementation of a reliable security system will take time. But while we have reached a particularly favorable moment in history, the gift of unlimited time has not been granted to us. We don't have years or months or even days to waste. Disaster stalks us and our mission to preserve ourselves and our planet becomes more urgent with every tick of the clock.

Although the world has changed radically since the end of the Cold War, a handful of nations retain their weapons of mass destruction, running the risks of miscalculation, catastrophic accident or that their weapons will not fall into the hands of political, sectarian or military extremists. While some have cut back on the number of weapons in their arsenals, many, including the U.S. have yet to ratify the Comprehensive Test Ban Treaty. They have yet to accept the simple truth that weapons of annihilation have no place in the strategic thinking of any nation.

A Commitment to Nuclear Abolition

The United States and the Russian Federation, the latter heir to most of the military power of the former Soviet Union, are the premier members of the nuclear club and they have taken a number of steps to back away from the nuclear terror. But they have not taken the most fundamental step. They haven't fully committed to the total elimination of all nuclear weapons, despite their obligations under Article VI of the Nuclear Non-Proliferation Treaty.

Such a commitment is a logical and necessary step toward the eventual establishment of a world ruled by enforceable law. It is a step that does not have to await the creation of global enforcement mechanisms. It can be taken with minimal delay and, because it depends on vision and commitment, it can bring the gift of nuclear weapons freedom to an imperiled world. By abolishing their own nuclear arsenals, the U.S., Russia and other nuclear club members not only could reduce the world's danger level, but they could set an example for every nation that considers itself an advocate of peace through genuine security.

Arguments against Abolition

For years, nuclear abolition was largely supported by members of the traditional peace movement. While a handful of politicians, military strategists and foreign policy specialists argued for abolition, an overwhelming majority of their colleagues in Washington, Moscow, London, Paris, Beijing and other capitals long have been united in their opposition. Their thinking starts with the belief that the nuclear threat was responsible for a half-century free of major conflicts. They contend that the existence of nuclear weapons continues to deter aggressive military action and restrain the leaders of renegade states. They credit nuclear deterrence with keeping the lid on global hot spots from the Middle East to the Korean Peninsula and beyond. They say the nuclear umbrella provided by the United States reduced proliferation by making it unnecessary for nations like Japan to pursue their own nuclear weapons program. They scoff at the notion that nations with nuclear capabilities ever will agree to dismantle all their weapons or that nations with secret nuclear programs will voluntarily write off their investment or close the door on what they see as an opportunity to achieve a balance of power with their enemies.

Opponents of abolition contend that there is no way to prevent cheating by any nation that signs an agreement calling for the dismantling of nuclear weapons. Besides, they argue, knowledge of nuclear weapons construction will continue to exist even if the weapons themselves are destroyed. So there always will be the possibility that a new generation of warheads sooner or later will appear.

Abolition opponents believe that in attempting to end the nuclear peril, the world will be stimulating an escalation in conventional weaponry. They believe a new arms race, one for superiority in conventional weapons, will increase international tensions and lead to the outbreak of armed conflict in locations that for years have been pacified by fear of the ultimate destruction of a nuclear attack. Those who oppose abolition cannot conceive of a world free of the nuclear threat. They sincerely believe the existence of these horrifying weapons contributes to international security. They endorse reductions in the size of the world's nuclear arsenals, but not their total elimination. They are likely to characterize those who hold a differing point of view, those who believe nuclear weapons threaten humanity's future, as inexperienced or naïve.

In my view, naiveté more fittingly characterizes the thinking of those who use the deterrent argument to support the continued possession of nuclear arms. America's overwhelming nuclear arsenal did not deter North Korea from invading the South nor North Vietnam from successfully overrunning South Vietnam. Britain's nuclear capability did not stop Argentina from invading the Falklands. Soviet nuclear weapons did not force Afghan rebels to abandon their cause. Saddam Hussein was not deterred from invading Kuwait by his certain knowledge that American tactical nuclear weapons could strike Baghdad in a matter of minutes.

Further, the existence of nuclear weapons did nothing to stem a massive conventional arms buildup that proceeded in parallel with a nuclear arms race of grotesque excess. In retrospect, a strong argument can be made that nuclear weapons prolonged and intensified the Cold War and that deterrence was simply a formula for unmitigated disaster, so aptly called MAD, mutually assured destruction.

Cracks in the Establishment's Unanimity

Post-1945 history clearly shows that nuclear weapons are ineffective as deterrents to war. If they are used against another nation that itself possesses nuclear weapons, devastating retaliation is a certainty. If they are used against a nonnuclear nation, the moral outrage of civilized society would be ruinous for the user. As a practical matter, it is impossible to conceive of a situation in which the employment of nuclear weapons would produce positive results. They serve no military or other purpose. Despite their enormous cost in brainpower, money and environmental problems, they are worthless.

Nonetheless, the defense and foreign policy establishment long has been nearly unanimous in its opposition to nuclear abolition. Only recently has the apparent unanimity started to show signs of cracking. Some members of the establishment, including many with impeccable credentials as nuclear warriors and strategists, have stepped forward to express their support for abolition at the earliest possible moment. In late 1996, for example, sixty retired generals and admirals from around the world joined in issuing a statement calling for additional nuclear arms cuts and the phased elimination of all nuclear weapons. The group included two former supreme allied commanders in Europe, the former chief of Britain's defense staff, and prominent Russian commanders.

Air Force General George Lee Butler, mentioned in the acknowledgments, was before his 1994 retirement in charge of the U.S. Strategic Command which oversees nuclear bombers and land and submarine launched nuclear missiles. He is one of the military leaders who, to use his words "... made the long and arduous intellectual journey from staunch advocate of nuclear deterrence to public proponent of nuclear abolition."

"Despite all of the evidence," General Butler has noted,

> we have yet to fully grasp the monstrous effects of these weapons. . . . [We continue Cold War policies and practices in a world] . . . where our security interests have been utterly transformed.
>
> As to those who believe nuclear weapons are desirable or inevitable, I would say these weapons exact a terrible price even if never used. Accepting nuclear weapons as the ultimate arbiter of conflict condemns the world to live under a dark cloud of perpetual anxiety. Worse, it codifies

mankind's most murderous instincts as an acceptable resort when other options for resolving conflict fail.

Another senior military commander to lend his prestige and support to the cause of denuclearization is Stansfield Turner, retired four-star admiral and former director of the Central Intelligence Agency. Turner has developed a "nuclear escrow" plan in which nuclear arsenals would be reduced to a level of perhaps 200 weapons and the remaining warheads and delivery vehicles would be separated and stored under international inspection. While not a formula for immediate nuclear abolition, Turner's innovative escrow plan would remove nuclear weapons from operational deployment and be a giant step toward their eventual elimination.

Other Voices for an Abolition Initiative

In a report issued in 1996, the prestigious Canberra Commission outlined a specific plan for eliminating nuclear weapons. The Commission, established in 1995 by the Australian government, declared that nuclear weapons pose an intolerable threat to all humanity, that the growing threats of nuclear proliferation and nuclear terrorism must be removed, that nuclear weapons diminish the security of all states and that states which possess them become themselves targets of nuclear weapons.

The Commission also added a hopeful note.

The opportunity now exists, perhaps without precedence or recurrence, to make a new and clear choice to enable the world to conduct its affairs without nuclear weapons and in accordance with the principles of the Charter of the United Nations. [Then the Commission called on the declared nuclear states—the United States, Russia, United Kingdom, France and China—to take the lead] . . . by committing themselves, unequivocally, to the elimination of all nuclear weapons. Such a commitment would propel the process (of nuclear abolition) in the most direct and imaginative way. All other governments must join this commitment and contribute to its fulfillment. . . . A nuclear weapons free world can be secured and maintained through political commitment and anchored in an enduring and binding legal framework.

As General Butler put it:

Notwithstanding the perils of transition in Russia, enmities in the Middle East, or the delicate balance of power in South and East Asia, I believe that a swelling chorus of reason and resentment will eventually turn the tide. As the family of mankind develops a capacity for collective outrage, so soon will it find avenues for collective action. The terror-filled anesthesia which numbed rational thought, made nuclear war thinkable, and grossly excessive arsenals possible during the Cold War is gradually wearing off. A renewed appreciation for the obscene power of a single nuclear weapon is taking a new hold on our consciousness, as we confront the nightmarish prospect of nuclear terror at the micro level.

Our Vulnerability to Nuclear Attack

Knowledge of how to build a nuclear device already is in the public domain and available to who knows how many tyrants, fanatics and crackpots. The materials needed to turn this knowledge into horrifying reality undoubtedly will become more and more available as older weapons are dismantled in a Russia beset by economic problems and besieged by corruption and gangsterism. In the not too distant future, homemade nuclear devices could replace the conventional bombs that have been detonated in such places as Saudi Arabia, London, Paris, and Oklahoma City. To deliver the new generation of relatively small but exceedingly powerful devices to the intended targets, a tyrant, fanatic or crackpot will not need a missile or high altitude bomber. The vehicle of choice well may be a truck, van or shipping container.

The limitations of our present ability to defend against nuclear attack—whether launched by terrorists or a hostile nuclear power—must not be used as an excuse for inaction. While we cannot erect a failproof shield, we can at least set an example for the family of nations. We can join with others in abolishing our own lethal stockpiles and in establishing the simple truth that possession of weapons of annihilation constitutes a crime against humanity.

The prospect of "nuclear terror at the micro level" is not a cloud on the distant horizon. It is here and now. It is a reality that must be confronted without delay. It is a threat that must be eliminated by a prompt world-wide commitment to abolish all nuclear weapons, a commitment, as the Canberra Commission put it, "anchored in an enduring and binding legal framework."

The Need for a Commitment to Abolish Nuclear Weapons

Unfortunately, the "enduring and binding legal framework" is not likely to be developed quickly. Old ways of thinking do not easily yield their power. So when the nuclear abolition issue makes its way to the top of America's agenda—and I pray it will happen in the very near future—its chances of success will depend not only on its own logic but on its positioning as an important step toward a comprehensive and enforceable system of international antiaggression and antiweapons laws.

A commitment to abolition will represent a major shift in U.S. policy so the debate in the halls of government and among individual citizens will be intense. Congress and the White House, politicians and pundits all will have their say. The policies of the past will be attacked and defended. Plans for the future will be praised and denounced. But as the arguments continue, I am convinced our policies will begin to change. Our national leadership in government and in many segments of the private sector will have begun to understand the necessity of turning away from the obsolete doctrines of the Cold War. They will begin to realize that the time has come for us to embark on a bold new course of action. This change of direction will not be radical at first. Discussion and compromise—hallmarks of democratic society—do not lend themselves to abrupt shifts in guiding principles. But subtly, carefully, the United States will lead the world toward a new level of peaceful, productive cooperation.

Moving Toward a Postnuclear Age

To begin with, the United States and like-minded nations will move with caution toward a system of truly nonprovocative defense. This will call for an accelerated schedule of reductions in the development and production of all weapons of mass murder as well as the abolition of all such weapons by a date certain. At the same time, the United States and its friends will continue to provide financial and technical resources needed to reduce the threat posed by the huge stockpiles of weapons and weapons materials in Russia.

While the United States and its friends reassert their opposition to aggression, they will maintain, perhaps even strengthen, their own defensive capabilities. They also will take the lead in a worldwide effort to curb and eventually abolish the arms trade. It is legitimate for the United States to produce the weapons it needs to defend itself and its allies against aggression. But I do not think it should be in the business of selling arms. Arms sales contribute to international rivalries, tensions and hostilities. If we are serious about putting an end to armed conflict, we ought to set an example for other industrialized nations by stopping the export of all military weapons, ammunition and equipment.

A positive step in this direction would be the adoption of an arms sales code of conduct barring weapons transfers to dictatorships and governments that commit aggression or abuse the human rights of their citizens. Legislation to this effect has been approved by the U.S. House of Representatives, although not the Senate. Such a code of conduct would begin to introduce standards of morality into the business of arms transfers and hopefully could pave the way for the abolition of weapons trafficking altogether.

Of course, there is money to be made in the arms industry. But it is blood money and its pursuit ought to be rejected on moral grounds. From my own experience in manufacturing, I see no persuasive reason for any company to persist in building arms. Production can be shifted to other products, probably with a greater potential for profit and certainly with less involvement in bureaucratic regulation. The arms trade thrives on international insecurity and it undermines the interests of international security.

We Need to Maintain Our Defenses

I fully understand that our arms sale policy always has emphasized helping our friends defend themselves and I see nothing wrong with the production of defensive arms that render offensive arms useless. The problem is defining the difference between defensive and offensive weapons. The F-16 is a good example. It is a superior machine for protecting a country's airspace but it is also capable of delivering a nuclear warhead. So is it a defensive or an offensive weapon? The answer for the F-16 or any other weapon depends not so much on the weapon itself but on the way it is used. So instead of wasting time debating definitions, we ought to concentrate on the long-term elimination of all weapons capable of inflicting devastating damage.

While we work for the day when such weapons have been erased from the face of the earth, we must continue to keep our guard up. We must assert our right to defend ourselves and our armed forces must be ready to meet and overcome a wide range of challenges. After all, there is nothing wrong with maintaining an appropriate level of defense. Every living creature has a defensive system, a fact underscored by the very existence of the creature. In human affairs, the existence of individuals and of nations depend on their ability to defend themselves. As a Hindu proverb puts it, "A man without a stick will be bitten even by a sheep."

By maintaining strong defenses while reducing their investment in new and redundant systems for the obliteration of the world's civilian population, the United States and like-minded nations will be strengthening, not abandoning, their commitment to democratic ideals. They will be moving toward a day when substantial, worldwide reductions in overall arms expenditures will become a reality. They will be freeing economic and intellectual resources that can be rechanneled into activities that will serve the best interests of Americans and people in every other nation.

Reactions to Our Leadership

The implementation by the United States of policies that represent a shift from our long-standing reliance on weapons of annihilation will produce mixed reactions in many nations. In Western and Central Europe, there will be concerns that the U.S. is abandoning its position of leadership and ignoring the possibility of a resurgence of territorial expansionism in Russia. In the Middle East, some will wonder if U.S.

actions will not encourage aggression by Iraq, Iran, or Syria. In the Far East, leaders of nations long protected by America's arms well might express concerns about the intentions of nuclear-armed China.

The fact of the matter is that the proposed new policies do involve some risk. But it is my experience that nothing of great value can be obtained without risk. It is an inevitable consequence of leadership. By facing up to risk, we can gain the Fourth Freedom for coming generations. By chancing a limited period of uncertainty and accepting the possibility of a modest amount of economic discomfort for a relatively short period of time, we can obtain limitless years of security. By any standard of judgment, the transaction will be one of history's greatest bargains.

Since the new policy of abolition is nonconfrontational, nondiscriminatory and offers all nations the opportunity to share in the benefits of a postnuclear age, the level of risk will be low. In the end, the concept of nuclear abolition will prevail—not necessarily because of universal agreement but because it has the endorsement of the U.S. Freed of excessive armaments expenditures, the U.S. economy will be reasserting itself as the creative driving force for the economies of the world. Self-interest will motivate many nations to join the United States in leading the world away from disaster.

In Russia, the new policy will be carefully analyzed by leaders who, in many cases, have not been able to move their thinking beyond the Cold War. They still harbor dreams of Russian ascendancy and, thanks to years of insularity and a tradition of suspecting U.S. intentions and motives, they are not likely to offer instant, enthusiastic cooperation. Besides, stirring up old images of hostility and confrontation might be a useful strategy for leaders struggling to retain control of a nation weakened by instability and discontent. Some Russian politicians may attempt to seek popularity by characterizing the new U.S. policy as a threat to their nation's future. They may seek to turn public opinion away from hope and toward fear.

Within America, opponents of the new policy will conjure up a frightening picture. They will warn that nuclear abolition amounts to national surrender. Those who support abolition will be vilified and demonized for their vision and courage. But if they stand fast, common sense will prevail and the American people will rally around a commitment that has as its objective the removal of weapons that can destroy any hope for the future.

A Step toward Reliable Law Enforcement

In opting for abolition, the U.S. will be joining other nations in a historic movement away from violence and, while abolition is not the end of the world's quest for effective international security, it could be the beginning of the end. Nuclear abolition is too important an accomplishment to be left unprotected. Its adoption not only will be a major milestone in humanity's establishment of a lawful world, but it also will necessitate establishment of the "enduring and binding legal framework" called for by the Canberra Commission.

The triumph of nuclear abolition will assure the ultimate triumph of the rule of law and give added momentum to efforts to create the enduring, dependable, nonviolent system of enforcement that will be the guarantor of Freedom from Fear. Through enlightened and relentless citizen support, plus a dash of creativity and statesmanship, the world of the Fourth Freedom will become a reality. Then we will understand that the information we have been uncovering in our search is nothing less than a blueprint for civilization's next age of progress.

CHAPTER TEN

Enhanced Security through Carrots and Sticks

Peace is never long preserved by weight of metal or by an armament race. Peace can be made tranquil and secure only by understanding and agreement fortified by sanctions. We must embrace international cooperation or international disintegration.

—Bernard M. Baruch

For years, many foreign policy specialists acted as if they doubted the ability of economic power to influence the behavior of a nation. They rarely considered the suitability of incentives and they seemed to view sanctions as a perfunctory step on the route from warning to war. While they occasionally were willing to suggest the imposition of sanctions, they consistently expressed reservations about adopting a course of action that conventional wisdom had branded futile.

Only in recent times have the foreign policy specialists had a change of heart. They have reviewed the evidence and they have discovered a number of significant cases demonstrating the potency of economic power in the regulation of international relationships. Many of them have come to the conclusion that sanctions and incentives, carefully planned and meticulously implemented, can achieve a broad range of foreign policy objectives.

Answering the "What If" Question

Unfortunately, a tradition of negative thinking about the value of economic power has not disappeared. The experts continue to downplay the effectiveness of the economic weapon. They have not broadened their horizons to see economics as the cornerstone of international security through world law. In responding to specific events, they tend to downplay the potential effectiveness of incentives and sanctions by identifying, or imagining, obstacles to their utilization.

The policymakers rely on their often flawed memories of what was rather than on the vision of what might be. Academicians, members of the foreign policy community, business executives and other opinion leaders often seem perfectly willing to ignore the many lessons of recent history. They appear to be more committed to their objections than to the possibilities that clearly exist. When you analyze these objections you'll find they are mostly built around what I have come to describe as the "what if" question:

"What if Japan won't join in sanctioning international lawbreakers?"

"What if France decides to go it alone?"

"What if any of our trading partners in Europe or on the Pacific Rim balk at sanctioning nations that refuse to eliminate weapons of mass destruction or decline to help fund the incentives that sometimes may be needed to establish a world at peace under the rule of law?"

The best answer to these and other what-ifs is another question:

Why would?

Why would Japan give up access to its best market and, at the same time, reject the umbrella of protection offered by the United States?

Why would France, devastated by two world wars, turn its back on a new opportunity to achieve international security?

Why would any trading partner of the United States reject an invitation to join in endorsing the international rule of law or in supporting the abolition of nuclear weapons? Why wouldn't a trading partner embrace the opportunity to take part in the development of a system that would provide protection from civilian-threatening weapons, end aggression, reduce terrorism and foster expanded economic development? Why would nations turn down a chance to lay down the heavy burden of aggressive armaments and enjoy the benefits of enhanced international trade?

Sanctions Have Positive Power

I know the what-ifs are asked in good faith. But in raising objections, the askers always seem to overlook the positive aspects of economic sanctions. They do not seem to realize that economic sanctions, used prudently, uniformly and without malice, can be effective in human relationships at every level, from the interpersonal to the international. Sanctions give support to words, often accomplishing what cannot be accomplished by words alone. Sanctions are a tool that can be used by any person or any organization that seeks to improve conditions that affect them. Sanctions can be mutually beneficial. They can help those who impose them and those against whom they are imposed. They contribute to social order by conferring nonviolent power on every individual and every organization.

Sanctions which take the form of the universal act of withholding have enormous potential in international affairs. But as the what-if questions indicate, skepticism sometimes makes it difficult for us to see that this potential can be realized, not in the distant future, but here and now.

There is nothing new about the use of sanctions in international relationships. They are as old as disputes between tribes or cities or kingdoms. The siege and the blockade have been part of military strategy from the beginning of human history. Both impose economic sanctions. The boycott is another example. By declining to purchase the goods produced by a target company, individuals always have been able to make their voices heard. They can change corporate policy, for example, force a multinational corporation to stop promoting the sale of infant formula in developing countries or coerce an oil company to open franchises to more individuals from minority groups.

The federal government effectively uses the threat of economic sanctions to enforce laws and regulations. If a state fails to build a highway to federal specifications, the U.S. Department of Transportation will withhold funds until the deficiencies are corrected. If a college or university fails to meet the standards established in civil rights or other legislation, the U.S. Department of Education will threaten to cut off the flow of federal dollars.

A Positive as Well as a Negative Side

Another everyday example of an effective economic sanction is the strike. By withholding or threatening to withhold services, labor can achieve gains that will strengthen its position at the bargaining table. The withholding of goods or services, either by an individual or a group, is the most frequently used and most productive negotiating strategy. It works because it is based on the existence of something desirable. This desirable something is the other, positive side of withholding, the incentive that encourages cooperation, the benefit that builds agreement.

In family relationships, the negative act of withholding draws its power from the desirability of positive acts of affection and support. In industry, a strike can work to show both labor and management the mutual benefit of continued efficient production. In international relationships, effective sanctions depend not so much on coercion as on an understanding of the rewards that belong to all nations that maintain their good standing in the worldwide trading community.

South Africa's Example

An example that comes to mind is the economic sanctions imposed on South Africa. The objective was to convince the government to change its racial policies. At first, the ruling authorities dug in their heels in opposition. But as the sanctions gained more and more support in the international community, the opposition faded and the objective finally was achieved.

Many factors were involved, of course, including the support given to sanctions by South Africa's majority population group. A key element in the successful imposition of sanctions was the pressure applied by international bankers. When major international banks decided in the mid-1980s to rollover loans short-term, in effect applying a freeze on long-term credit to the apartheid regime, business executives and government leaders in South Africa were forced to take notice. As a result, some of South Africa's economic and political leaders began to urge a change in the racial policies that had been condemned by civilized society.

At the risk of oversimplifying the issue, let me also suggest that sanctions were effective in South Africa not just because they directly affected powerful individuals and institutions or because they enjoyed internal support or because they created economic problems on a broad scale but because they reminded the nation's leadership of all that could be gained once the barriers to trade were lifted.

Why Not a Nonviolent Approach to Global Law?

The successful utilization in South Africa of the power of withholding and the implicit power to give was hailed around the world as a triumph of nonviolent enforcement of acceptable standards of behavior. Then it began to dawn on many that a mixture of carrots and sticks is almost always a part of successful diplomacy. Carrots and sticks, rewards and penalties, can change attitudes and policies within a target nation. If the nation's leaders feel the pain of the stick and, at the same time, see the benefits that are close at hand, they are more likely to comply with the demands made on them.

The lesson is unmistakable. Sanctions and incentives can be used to enforce the will of the international community. It does not take a giant leap of faith to believe sanctions and incentives also can be used to secure the global rule of law encompassing nuclear abolition, elimination of all other weapons of mass destruction and the end of armed aggression, state-sponsored terrorism and other crimes against humanity.

Failure of the League of Nations

Unfortunately, the employment of carrots and sticks, incentives and sanctions, on a broad scale still has a bad name with some political scientists and historians, and their students. They cite examples of failed sanctions policies. But, in my view, the blame must be assigned not to the policies but to those responsible for transforming them into action. For example, during the decades after World War I, the use of sanctions was authorized by the Covenant of the League of Nations. League members were expected to impose sanctions on any nation that disturbed the peace. They were supposed to establish a blockade of the aggressor nation's frontiers and to boycott the aggressor's products. To minimize the hardship on nations imposing sanctions, League members were expected to help one another. It was a powerful idea and with prompt, coordinated action by nations professing League membership, it might have put an end to war long before the Manhattan Project released the nuclear terror.

Then the idea was tested in the real world of international politics. In 1931, Japan invaded the Chinese province of Manchuria. League members scolded Japan and condemned its aggression. They did little else. So Japan consolidated its conquest and, in a gesture of contempt for nations too timid to back their words with actions, withdrew from the League. In 1935, Mussolini's Italy invaded Ethiopia. This act of aggression was an unmistakable violation of the League Covenant and it triggered a flurry of activity. For a short time, it appeared that there would be prompt, coordinated action, that economic sanctions would be imposed against Italy and assistance would be directed to Ethiopia.

Public opinion was outspoken in its condemnation of the Italian attack on one of the world's weakest and most defenseless states. But public opinion failed to win the support of the governments that could have made sanctions effective. Both France and Britain dragged their feet. The United States, which had declined to become a League member, banned shipments of arms to both Italy and Ethiopia. But trade in other goods was allowed to continue. In fact, as Robin Renwick has pointed out in a report published by the Center for International Affairs, "The United States, which had supplied 6.5 percent of Italy's oil, was supplying 17.8 percent by the end of the year." Without the support of France and Britain—and with the United States providing Italy with an increasing share of the oil needed by its invading army—the League's sanctions lacked decisive impact and nations large and small abandoned the effort.

Sanctions and the United Nations

At the end of World War II, when the United Nations Organization was created, there was renewed support for sanctions as a peacekeeping alternative. A provision for sanctions was built into the UN charter. However, implementation required unanimous consent of the Security Council, a body that soon found itself crippled by vetoes or the threat of vetoes.

Indeed, as long as the veto power remains intact, the UN's ability to impose sanctions will be severely limited. It simply isn't realistic to expect a Security Council member to vote in favor of sanctions on itself or on one of its allies no matter how reprehensible its behavior. The veto, a concession to an outmoded understanding of national interests, effectively short-circuited much of the peacekeeping power of the UN during the years of U.S.-Soviet confrontation and continues to present an obstacle that must be eliminated at the earliest possible moment.

Even with the veto power in place, the post–Cold War period has witnessed a striking increase in international cooperation. Between 1990 and 1995, while the Security Council was adopting some 150 resolutions, the veto was used only twice and neither of the two vetoes were in opposition to sanctions. James C. Ngobi, secretary of the United Nations Sanctions Committee, has reported in an essay in *Economic Sanctions: Panacea or Peacebuilding in a Post–Cold War World?* edited by David Cortright and George A. Lopez, (Westview Press, Boulder, Colorado, 1995) that, "In the first 45 years of its existence, the United Nations imposed mandatory sanctions only twice. Since 1990, the Security Council has used sanctions at least six times to regulate and redress the accepted norms of behavior among nations through peaceful means." More recently, the number of cases of multilateral sanctions since the Cold War has risen to ten.

Incentives Can Enhance Security

Multinational sanctions, usually under the auspices of the Security Council, have been imposed on Iraq, the former Yugoslavia, Libya, Liberia, Somalia, Haiti, parts of Angola and Cambodia, Rwanda, Burundi, and Sierra Leone. In addition, incentives, the other side of sanctions, have been used effectively to reduce the nuclear peril related to the fragmentation of what was the Soviet Union. For example, thanks to the Cooperative Threat Reduction (CTR) program created in 1991 through legislation sponsored by U.S. Senators Sam Nunn, D-Georgia, and Richard Lugar, R-Indiana, Russia has increased ability to handle the so-called "loose nukes" problem. More than 2,000 nuclear warheads have been eliminated and hundreds of

ICBM silos and missile launchers have been destroyed. CTR also has helped remove more than 2,500 warheads from delivery vehicles, relocated nuclear weapons from Kazakhstan and Ukraine to within the borders of Russia and reduced the number of Russian nuclear storage sites.

Incentives played a major role in bringing about the October 1994 Agreed Framework that cracked open the door to the possibility of settling long-standing security issues on the Korean Peninsula. The United States, Japan and South Korea agreed to supply North Korea with heavy fuel oil, two power-generating nuclear reactors unlikely to yield weapons-grade nuclear materials and the promise of negotiations designed to end a half-century of armed North-South confrontation. For its part, North Korea agreed to put its nuclear weapons program on hold.

Since the Agreed Framework was signed, North Korea occasionally has alarmed both its neighbors and perceived enemies by test firing ballistic missiles, digging mysterious tunnels, sending spy submarines into South Korea's territorial waters and other provocative acts. It also has been negotiating the sale of its advanced missile technology to Iran. Yet, despite its willingness to rattle our cage, Pyongyang has earned high marks for living up to its commitments under the Agreed Framework. Its nuclear program has been halted and it appears to be moving toward the opening of its underground facilities to international inspectors.

Although the United States, Japan and South Korea have fallen behind in living up to their side of the agreement—for example, deliveries of fuel oil and construction of the new reactors are behind schedule—the Agreed Framework still stands. Thanks to incentives and the possibility that economic sanctions against North Korea will be relaxed, the possibility of greater security has been strengthened. Both sides have shown increased willingness to discuss divisive issues and, for the first time in decades, there is hope for the cooperation that will end the threat of hostilities once and for all.

Sanctions Achieve Success

Even with the inconsistent, fragmented and often inept incentives and sanctions efforts of the post–World War I and Cold War eras, the record is far more positive than many critics would have us believe. The Washington-based Institute for International Economics has studied

116 sanctions episodes between 1914 and 1990, carefully analyzing goals and results. The conclusion: 34 percent of the sanctions were successful in achieving their declared goals. The success rate compares favorably with that achieved through the use of military force but with less direct cost and without the slaughter, destruction and hatred that are inevitable consequences of military action.

An objective review of the evidence should demonstrate to even the most skeptical observer that international sanctions—carefully conceived, adequately supported and implemented with an even hand—have worked in the past and, with the cooperation of the world community, will work in the future.

Shortcomings of Unilateral Economic Action

The evidence also shows that sanctions rarely can be effective if they are imposed unilaterally. In today's interconnected, global economy, sanctions must be multilateral and, in my opinion, they also must be directed at both the nation that violates an accepted standard of behavior and its accomplices in crime. Unilateral sanctions, especially those directed at a violator but not against those continuing to trade with the violator, are destined to fail. When nation A withholds products from nation B, nations C and D too often are prepared to provide substitute sources for whatever has been withheld.

Cuba provides an instructive example. When Fidel Castro came to power, more than 75 percent of his nation's trade was with the United States. When the United States imposed its embargo, Cuba shifted its trade to the Soviet Union and its allies. In addition, the Soviets provided economic assistance in the amount of $2 to $3 billion annually. With the rejection of Communism and the recognition of economic problems in most of the nations of the former Soviet Union, the subsidy to Cuba dwindled and so did much of Cuba's trade with what had been the Soviet bloc. But other nations, including many of America's closest friends, filled the gap. And these nations objected strenuously in 1996 when the U.S. strengthened its sanctions in ways that were seen as harmful to at least some of Cuba's trading partners.

Much of the same pattern appeared in 1980 when the U.S. sought to punish the Soviet Union for its invasion of Afghanistan by boycotting the

Olympic Games and withholding shipments of wheat. While the firmness of U.S. opposition may have caused Soviet leaders to rethink any plans for other military adventures, it did not force the Soviets into immediate retreat. They were able to obtain adequate supplies of grain from other sources and, to this day, some of my farmer friends believe the principal loser was American agriculture.

Success Requires Consistency

Now it is easy to blame our allies for the failures of our go-it-alone policies. But we also must remember that without the solid support of a fully accepted international rule of law, it is tempting for leaders to vacillate rather than act, to ignore acts of aggression, to wish away threats to global security. In addition, U.S. policy rarely has been consistent enough to inspire the confidence of its friends or to frighten its enemies. When we have been consistent, we have succeeded to a remarkable degree. For example, when we joined with our allies in a long-term effort to impede the flow of advanced technology to the Soviet bloc, we dealt a severe blow to our Cold War adversaries.

By withholding high speed computers, advanced software and other tools of modern industry, we substantially raised the cost to the Soviets of their high priority effort to keep pace with the military developments of the West. At the same time, the embargo on technology transfers made it difficult for Soviet industry to satisfy the needs of private citizens. The strain on the Soviet economy and the dissatisfaction of the Soviet people—both exacerbated by the West's determination to stop the eastward flow of technology—helped spark the events that continue to shake the world. Indeed, the withholding of technology by the U.S. and its allies should be ranked as one of history's most successful exercises in the use of sanctions.

Taking Advantage of Interdependence

If only we could see the window of opportunity created by growing international awareness and economic interdependence. Today the interests of all nations are intertwined as never before. No nation can afford to be cut off from trade with other nations. No nation can long withstand an embargo on the manufactured goods it needs to satisfy the needs and aspirations of its people.

In simpler times, it might have been possible for a nation to achieve, or at least come close to, self-sufficiency. But that age now is long past. People in all parts of the world desire access to the fruits of technology. They seek the higher standard of living that is a result of technological advancement. They will not perpetually tolerate a government that prevents them from enjoying what they view as "the good life." In the present age of global trade and global communication, economic sanctions and incentives can be routinely effective in promoting and sustaining international security. Through the judicious use of economic power as a persuasive force, the United States can work with other nations to the benefit of all nations. It can achieve genuine national and international security and move the world into the civilized era of the Fourth Freedom.

New Route to a Lawful World

To be successful in this most worthwhile endeavor, the world's law-abiding nations will have to do away with their false fears. They will have to have faith, remembering that they are dealing from a position of strength, that their goal is neither political nor material, that they are acting solely in the service of this generation and those that follow.

The alternative is to continue to tolerate the presence of nuclear, biological and chemical weapons, to passively accept the spending of billions of dollars on weapons that can never guarantee lasting peace, to ignore the threat posed by international terrorists. Such a course of action, or inaction, surely is unacceptable to Americans and all others who care about themselves, their tradition of freedom and the future of their society. I believe those who care constitute a majority in America and around the world.

But they must become aware of the new road we have been exploring, a road that leads to a lawful world through the employment of economic rather than military power. When people understand that this road offers a practical, realistic approach to the solution of an ancient problem, they will make the right choices. They will choose development over destruction, competition over conquest, hope over fear, life over death.

CHAPTER ELEVEN

Targeted Economic Power Gets Results

The struggle to maintain peace is immeasurably more difficult than any military operation.

—Anne O'Hare McCormick

Rarely has the contrast between military power and economic power been so starkly illuminated as in the turmoil that turned the world's attention to Yugoslavia during the final years of the twentieth century.

Military power, utilized at first by rival groups within Yugoslavia and then by the North Atlantic Treaty Organization, has killed or wounded thousands of civilians, uprooted tens of thousands of families, created a refugee problem of immense scope and complexity, damaged or destroyed roads, bridges, airports, railroads, communications systems, electrical grids and other infrastructure facilities, changed the ethnic composition of the population in region after region, threatened the stability of nearby countries, guaranteed the deployment of peacekeeping troops for a prolonged period and perpetuated the false and corrosive beliefs that violence can play a constructive role in international affairs and that might makes right.

Military power has shown no signs of contributing to the establishment of a long-term climate of security in Yugoslavia or adjoining Balkan nations. Instead, the use of the military has made a difficult situation far more difficult. It has intensified human suffering, struck a crushing blow at Yugoslavia's economy and opened or reopened psy-chological scars that will not be healed for generations. It has cost Yugo-slavia and the NATO nations, principally the United States, billions of dollars and set the stage for a rebuilding effort that will cost billions more over many years.

On the other hand, when economic power was utilized by the United Nations in Yugoslavia in the early part of the decade, it produced no catastrophe of any kind. In fact, according to a report issued by a UN-convened conference meeting in Copenhagen, the multilateral sanctions with their inherent promise of reward were ". . . remarkably effective." The report, drafted after a careful review of the sanctions regime, went on to declare that UN sanctions ". . . *modified the behavior of the Serbian party to the conflict and may well have been the single most important reason for the government in Belgrade changing its policies and accepting a negotiated peace agreement in Dayton. . . ."*

Ignoring a Sanctions Success

In other words, economic power helped compel enemies to sit down at the negotiating table and reach agreement. It contributed to the less-ening of a serious threat to peace and security. It aided in halting violence in Bosnia, providing an opportunity for people to begin reconstructing their communities and their lives.

Although the lesson was clear, it was ignored by the bomb-obsessed leaders of the United States, the United Kingdom and at least some of their NATO allies. They allowed a successful UN sanctions program to be lifted soon after the signing of the Dayton accords. With only a half-hearted arms embargo still in effect and his legitimacy confirmed at Day-ton, Slobodan Milosevic felt free to pursue another one of his goals by stepping up attacks designed to drive ethnic Albanians out of Kosovo. While the U.S. did block Serb-controlled Yugoslavia from entering the International Monetary Fund, there was little or no attempt to target financial sanctions against Milosovic and his Serbian leadership clique. Even an oil embargo, an action that would have had a direct effect on the Serbian war machine, appears not to have been discussed until after our bombs had begun the systematic destruction of Yugoslavia.

What a tragedy. Instead of imposing sanctions and ratcheting them up to enforce the will of the world community, instead of making clear the possibility of incentives in return for constructive behavior, instead of building on the lessons learned so recently in the same part of the world, we chose to impose our will through military force. We had unmistakable evidence that sanctions work but we ignored it.

What We Learned

As the Security Council's experiment with economic power was succeeding in Yugoslavia, some essential elements were made evident:

1. *The Security Council's sanctions program was based on international law.* The United Nations Charter authorizes the Council to act on behalf of the international community whenever there is a threat to international peace and security.
2. *Security Council members acted in concert to authorize the imposition of sanctions.* While some members, notably the Russian Federation, were reluctant to sanction the Serbs, vetoes were not invoked and agreements were reached.
3. *Regional organizations worked together to achieve compliance.* Cooperating within the framework of the Organization for Security and Cooperation in Europe (OSCE) were such organizations and institutions as the European Union (EU), the Western European Union (WEU), NATO and the International Conference on the Former Yugoslavia.
4. *Nations bordering the former Yugoslavia were assisted in their enforcement efforts by the international community.* Customs officers from member nations of the OSCE were utilized by the border nations and, as early as 1992, Sanctions Assistance Missions (SAMS) were operating in Bulgaria, Hungary and Romania.
5. *The office of International Sanctions Coordinator was established to oversee the implementation of sanctions.* The office, the first of its kind, coordinated the efforts of national governments as well as regional and international organizations.
6. *The international community demonstrated patience.* The sanctions program against Yugoslavia began in 1991 and basically was kept in place

until 1996 when many of the desired results appeared to be within reach.

7. *Attention was paid to safeguarding the interests of the civilian population.* Food, medicine, clothing and other essentials of life were allowed through the blockade and the enforcement agencies worked in close cooperation with the International Red Cross and other humanitarian organizations.

A Complicated Project

It's important to remember that the application of sanctions to Yugoslavia was a complex undertaking. It involved a region with a long history of tension and instability, a part of the world where major powers have tested their strength for generations. But because of the catalytic influence of the Security Council, these powers found themselves working together to defuse a threat that in earlier days might have plunged much of Europe into war.

It's worth noting that the Security Council provided direction and coordination but, to a large degree, it depended on regional organizations to furnish needed personnel. The Security Council also was sensitive to the special needs of the nations that, thanks to the dictates of geography, found themselves on the front lines in the sanctioning-enforcement effort.

None of this was easy. Enforcing the embargo against the former Yugoslavia necessitated the development of working definitions of what was or was not contraband, what products could be allowed to pass through a checkpoint, which goods were clearly for civilian purposes and which could be used by the troops and irregulars involved in the fighting. Enforcement required the inspection of truck and train shipments at border crossings, the interdiction of freighters on the Adriatic and control of riverboats and barges on the Danube waterway. The identity, origin and destination of each shipment had to be checked and verified and so did the registry of each vessel bound for a port providing access to the former Yugoslavia. Attempts to circumvent the embargo had to be overcome. Smugglers, some of them operating with at least the tacit approval of local authorities, had to be outsmarted.

In addition to the embargo, the sanctions also banned air travel to and from the Federal Republic of Yugoslavia, maintenance of the Republic's aircraft, competition in sports, scientific and technical cooperation and cultural exchanges. Nations were authorized to freeze funds belonging to Yugoslavia and make sure they were made available to pay for humanitarian supplies, not to benefit Yugoslavian authorities.

A Wide Range of Cooperation

The experienced customs officers supplied by OSCE member nations played a key role in maintaining the integrity of the embargo. So did the boats that operated as the Danube Patrol Mission that was organized by cooperating regional organizations, and the naval vessels provided by WEU and NATO that helped in diverting maritime traffic to Italian and Albanian ports where cargoes could be inspected. While the use of force by the crews of the patrol craft was authorized, it never was required.

In addition to on-the-scene personnel and equipment, a Sanctions Assistance Missions Communications Centre (SAMCOMM) was established in Brussels. With a staff of twenty-six, including customs, information and budget specialists, SAMCOMM helped coordinate operations involving a number of nations, organizations and agencies with enforcement responsibilities covering many locations in and around the former Yugoslavia. SAMCOMM helped increase the effectiveness of the embargo effort by providing a continuing source of unifying information. It also helped keep the United Nations Sanctions Committee and the EU/OSCE Sanctions Liaison Group up to date on activities in the field.

Civilized Society Can Enforce the Law

Let me emphasize that I have provided only a partial description of the mechanics involved in the successful implementation of sanctions in the former Yugoslavia. I also have chosen not to attempt to describe the international political maneuvering and the diplomatic triumphs and disappointments that are related to the sanctioning effort. I did not want a complicated recitation of history to get in the way of a very simple message. So I cited only a part of the operational record—most of it gleaned from the report of the Copenhagen conference—to make a point: *When civilized society has the will, it will find a way.*

In this instance, civilized society was appalled by the barbarism of the conflict involving Serbs, Croats and Bosnians. The hatreds expressed through ethnic cleansing, mass rape and genocidal killing and revealed to the world through television and other mass media, were repugnant to the people of the world. When the problem persisted, everyday individuals demanded action by their national leaders. So working through the Security Council, civilized society sought to end the fighting and restore stability. A principal part of the strategy was a sanctions program. But, as the Copenhagen report indicates, ". . . the instrument of sanctions is still relatively undeveloped and blunt, mainly because it has only been applied on a limited number of occasions, mostly after the end of the Cold War."

The Security Council had little experience in the imposition of sanctions. There were few precedents for many of the tactics involved in implementing the sanctions strategy. There was no comprehensive manual of procedures, no roadmap into a territory that was largely unknown, no wealth of experience that could be drawn on to get a sanctions regime up and running. Yet, it happened. Not perfectly, of course, but effectively enough to make a difference, not only in the former Yugoslavia, but in building a case for the greater use of economic power in the pursuit of peace, justice and security.

Learning from Experience

As I have been emphasizing, this power is not just one of many tools in the kit available to a world committed to the suppression of violence. By its nature and universality, economic power has the potential to become the preeminent agent for the establishment and enforcement of the rule of law. While economic power may have been ignored or underused in the past, it is gaining credibility and acceptance. The experience in the former Yugoslavia demonstrates that when incentives and sanctions are used with commitment and intelligence they can play a key role in making the rule of law a reality.

From the successes and shortcomings of the actions in the Yugoslavia theater, the world should now understand a number of facts. Imposition of sanctions must be based on a plan of action that is in place and on procedures that are widely understood and accepted. Definitions of humanitarian aid, contraband materials and products, monetary transfers, transshipments of goods and other subjects must be complete, concise and easily understood.

In addition, the Security Council must be equipped to direct and coordinate sanctioning operations and to utilize the specialized assistance available from national governments and regional organizations and institutions. The cooperation of these governments and organizations must be sought and obtained as early as possible. The need to help nations bordering a sanctions target must be recognized from the start. These nations may require assistance in enforcing an embargo and in compensating for hardships caused by a shutdown in bilateral trade.

The Yugoslavia sanctions were effective in large part because the nations of Europe made a special commitment to provide experienced, competent enforcement personnel. European regional organizations, acting under the authority of the United Nations Security Council, took responsibility for monitoring and enforcing the sanctions. This could be an important model for future sanctions programs because it demonstrates how regional cooperation can contribute to the success of UN authorized sanctions.

Easing the Hardship of Civilians

In addition, every effort must be made to minimize the suffering of the everyday citizens of a target nation. It simply is not fair for innocent civilians to pay a high price for the mistakes and misdeeds of those directly responsible for the conduct of government. Besides, if innocent civilians suffer, the concept of sanctions will be discredited in the eyes of the world community.

This happened in Iraq. After the Gulf War, Saddam Hussein pinned the blame for civilian hardship on the UN-imposed shutdown on oil exports. Iraqi officials claimed the embargo left them without the money needed to buy medical supplies and equipment and they backed their claim with televised photos of suffering children. The Security Council offered to provide humanitarian relief but it did little to counter Saddam Hussein's propaganda. The UN failed to explain to the Iraqis that their problems stemmed from the criminal behavior of their leaders. The UN also did not adequately communicate the fact that Iraq's leadership elite continued to prosper despite the oil sale embargo. As a result, Saddam Hussein's propaganda scored a victory. The result was an outpouring of sympathy from around the world and an undeserved black eye for the sanctions concept.

If Iraqi leaders were genuinely interested in obtaining humanitarian assistance for their people, they would not have delayed acceptance of the UN's oil for food program for five years. This program, outlined in Security Council Resolution 986, permitted oil sales for the purchase of food and medicine for the Iraqi people and to pay for Gulf War compensation claims and UN operations in Iraq. Under oil for food, revenues from Iraqi oil sales have been deposited in a UN account at the Banque de Paris. This innovative arrangement has prevented Saddam Hussein from getting his hands on the money, and insures that the funds are used solely to provide food, medical supplies, and related humanitarian goods.

As I said before, if there is a will, there is a way. If the civilized world is committed to protect civilians, it will discover a system for doing just that. It goes without saying that such safeguards are not available when the instrument for enforcing international law is military force. It does not lend itself to civilian-protecting restrictions. Bombs are meant to be destructive and there is no way to guarantee that the destruction will be limited to military personnel and equipment.

A "Smart Sanctions" Strategy

On the other hand, economic power can be targeted and controlled. Indeed, so-called "smart sanctions" are at the heart of a new strategy that is emerging at the United Nations and among at least some U.S. foreign affairs specialists. Instead of sweeping sanctions that may have cruel consequences for ordinary citizens, smart sanctions exert coercive pressure against the decision makers responsible for breaking international law. Smart sanctions are targeted to hit specific individuals and groups through financial restrictions, arms embargoes and travel bans.

Financial restrictions can be used by the community of nations to deny criminal leaders access to a vital resource—hard currency. Through cooperative action, coordinated by the United Nations, the criminals would be prevented from obtaining the cash they need to retain or strengthen their grip on power. They would find it increasingly difficult to hide their money, even in unregulated, offshore financial institutions. Their ability to transfer assets to sheltered locations would be limited. No longer would these criminal leaders be free to enhance the financial position of themselves and their families while they continue to flout the rule of international law.

Arms embargoes, rigorously monitored and consistently enforced, are a form of selective sanctions that can reduce the real or potential level of violence. They are classified as targeted sanctions because they primarily affect the military while avoiding harmful economic effects on civilians. It's evident that without the availability of weapons, conflicts are unlikely to escalate into wars. But for an arms embargo to achieve the desired results, international cooperation must be strong and resolute. National governments must be prepared to work together. They must be willing to enforce the embargo among their citizens and on companies operating within their borders. Nations must make it clear that they will not tolerate any attempt to sell or transport arms in violation of an embargo imposed by the Security Council. The Security Council itself must provide strong, reliable and impartial leadership.

Travel bans already have been utilized on a limited scale by the Security Council. It has restricted air travel to and from a targeted nation and it has restricted the travel of targeted individuals. As with other targeted sanctions, travel bans largely affect the ruling elite of a nation and have minimal humanitarian impact on everyday citizens. A travel ban can help isolate leaders who are guilty of criminal conduct. It brands them as lawbreakers and erodes their legitimacy in their own nation and abroad.

Patience and Resolve Are Essential

No matter what form they take, economic incentives and sanctions do not produce instantaneous results. They are not a quick cure for lawlessness. They require time for their effect to be felt at the leadership levels of a target nation. Unfortunately, patience sometimes can be misinterpreted as indecision. When that happens, when there is real or imagined uncertainty on the part of the sanctioning body, the usefulness of sanctions will be dealt a serious, perhaps fatal, blow.

The remedy for this problem is a large dose of resolve by the sanctioners. They must decide at the outset exactly the scope of the incentives and sanctions program they intend to impose. The sanctioning body also must develop a clear understanding of its objectives. Then it must stick to its position. It must not give a misleading impression by stepping back from a confrontation. It must avoid the temptation to weaken the sanctions before they have had a full opportunity to do their work. The sanctioners must be steadfast in their commitment or they will be cutting the ground from under themselves.

In business, I learned that there are times when the only way to deal with a recalcitrant distributor or supplier is to act decisively. To achieve a legitimate business objective, to get some people to live up to a contract or perform up to standard, it occasionally becomes necessary to, as the saying goes, "cut off their water." If this is done resolutely and if sufficient time is provided for a thoughtful response, the sanctioning process inevitably will succeed.

In international affairs, lack of resolve and a shortage of patience help account for the apparent failure of a number of sanctions efforts. But there is another, perhaps more significant reason. We simply have not got it through our heads that economic power is the most influential agent in society. It is not a poor cousin of military power. It is not something that ought to be thought of as a temporary or interim enforcement step. It is not a less desirable, but perhaps more agreeable, substitute for armed intervention. It is not a sugar-coated pill to be swallowed by politicians who want to immunize themselves against the effects of their own timidity. It is the tool that can change the world, the instrument that can give us the security and protection of the international rule of law.

Assuring Cooperation with Sanctions

As the Copenhagen report suggests, economic power can assist in bringing about conformance with the law. Through voluntary agreement, nations joined in an effort to use sanctions to confine a conflict to a limited geographic area. But what about the possibility of defections? What if some nations decline to take part in a civilized approach to law enforcement?

Given the present state of affairs, defections could have a devastating effect not only on sanctions, but on an entire peace process. The breaking of ranks by a major player in international trade, the decision by a nation to continue trading with the target nation, would make the imposition of effective sanctions difficult if not impossible. So if the world is to rely on sanctions, it must find a way to assure broad cooperation with a sanctions regime.

Under the UN Charter, member states are required to comply with Security Council resolutions. International law demands mandatory cooperation. But many nations fail to comply with Security Council resolutions and are either unable or unwilling to cooperate in the enforcement of sanctions. Some member states willfully violate UN resolutions. At present there are no penalties for such behavior. If international law is to have force, mandatory cooperation should be enforced. Countries that refuse to cooperate with sanctions should be punished. They also should be compelled to pay the price. Like the target nation, they should be subjected to sanctions. They should be punished as accomplices in crime.

The idea of punishing both criminals and those who assist them is commonplace in the laws of individual nations. It is rarely discussed within the framework of international law. Yet, I would argue that it makes such good sense that it must be included in the system of world law and law enforcement that we have been striving to identify.

When such a system is in place, there will be no doubt about what constitutes criminal activity. When sanctions are imposed, all nations will understand their duty. If some choose to turn their backs on the will of civilized society, they will be treated as the lawbreakers they are. Law-abiding nations, and I believe the United States will be among them, will use their economic leverage to protect the world from outlaws and their sympathizers. For the first time, the world will have a nonviolent way of dealing with nations that violate civilized norms.

The difference between the present and the future, the gap between today's largely hit or miss system and the regularized system we have been uncovering, is a measurement of the work that remains to be accomplished. But there is reason for optimism, not discouragement. We already have come a great distance. The carrots and sticks of incentives and sanctions have proven their worth in the life and death setting of an international crisis in the Balkans. The limitations and liabilities of military force have been repeatedly and conclusively demonstrated. We are moving closer to the age in which we and our children can walk with confidence into the adventures and opportunities that are humanity's heritage.

CHAPTER TWELVE

Turning to the Security Council

Internationalism does not mean the end of individual nations. Orchestras don't mean the end of violins.

—Golda Meir

To anyone who is serious about preventing armed aggression and eliminating weapons of mass murder, the case for world law is compelling. Only the rule of law can provide assurance of long-term compliance with civilized standards of behavior and, while I strongly believe in the importance of voluntary action, I fear it is too fragile a vessel for the hopes of the world.

But if we agree on the necessity of world law, we also must identify an effective instrument of enforcement. There are two possibilities. The first is to establish a new agency empowered to enforce the law, perhaps with its own police force. The new agency would start with a clean slate. It would be free of the baggage of the past and able to get a fresh start at building the confidence of the world's nations. But, as a practical matter, would nations be willing to gamble their future security on an agency that is unknown and untested? Could they agree on the mission and structure of a new agency? Or would such a proposal only lead to prolonged arguments that would put a permanent roadblock in the path of enforcement?

Security Council Problems and Potential

That brings us to the second possibility: turn over enforcement to an existing agency. The logical choice is the Security Council of the United Nations. While the Security Council has not earned a five-star rating for effectiveness, it has some positive attributes. The most important is the fact that it already has a charter to enforce peace among the nations of the world. With the Security Council, there will be no need to start from scratch. It doesn't need authorization. It already has it. However, even the most dedicated UN supporters agree that the Security Council rarely has lived up to the expectations of its creators. In crisis after crisis, it has failed to act. On issue after issue, it has missed the chance to provide leadership.

The universally acknowledged problem is the veto. Any one of the five permanent Security Council members—United States, China, Russia, Britain and France—has the power to block any proposed enforcement action. Each has the ability to use its veto to safeguard its own national interests or the interests of one of its clients or allies. The result has been decades of disappointment and frustration. Even worse, the ineffectiveness of the Security Council may have convinced a generation that cooperation and coordination are beyond humanity's reach.

Like nearly everyone who longs for the establishment of a world ruled by law, I deplore the shortcomings of the Security Council. I believe the world would be a better place if the veto had not shortcircuited dozens of well-intended security initiatives. But I also am a realist. When it comes to international security, the Council is the only game in town. Its veto power cannot be wished away. It is a reality that must be dealt with and the sooner we get started, the better off our world will be.

How the Veto Came to Be

To begin with, we have to recognize that the veto may have been an essential ingredient in the recipe that produced the United Nations. As the UN Charter was being drafted during the closing days of World War II, nuclear bombs had not been detonated over Hiroshima or Nagasaki. No one seemed capable of envisioning the long-term effect of a new class of weapons profoundly more devastating than anything in the history of warfare. Because the nuclear threat was unknown or underrated, the necessity of creating a strong Security Council was not as obvious as it is to us today. What was obvious was a growing atmosphere of fear and suspicion that was eroding relationships among the nations moving toward victory over Germany and Japan. The victors did not share the same vision of the future. The hot war was not over when the Cold War started to take its place. Despite statements of continuing solidarity by the Soviet Union, the U.S. and other allies, distrust was beginning to make itself felt across Europe and Asia. So while governments agreed on the necessity of an international security agency to prevent another war, they were reluctant to surrender the authority that would assure the agency's effectiveness. To secure at least the nominal participation of the five major powers, each was granted the right to derail any proposal that seemed in any way a threat to its policies, perogatives and perceived national interests.

Without the veto provision in the UN Charter, the Security Council may never have come into existence. Without the Security Council, shortcomings and all, the United Nations would be little more than an international debating society.

During the Cold War, of course, the Security Council repeatedly was paralyzed by the veto. With arrays of nuclear weapons targeted at each other, the superpowers were afraid to move from confrontation to conciliation. They were frozen into positions that prevented them from taking the smallest steps to prevent aggression. Each supported its friends unconditionally. Each used the Security Council as a pulpit from which to preach its message to friends, foes and those professing neutrality.

Security Council Accomplishments

On the rare occasions when the superpowers shared an interest in keeping the peace, the Security Council demonstrated its potential. UN peacekeepers helped suppress violence between Greeks and Turks on Cyprus, saved civilian lives in the Congo (later Zaire), maintained buffer zones between Israel, Egypt and Syria and supervised the withdrawal of Israeli forces from southern Lebanon.

In the 1990s with the Cold War over, the Security Council seemed ready to assume the role envisioned for it by its founders. When Iraq invaded

Kuwait, the Security Council responded by imposing sanctions, setting a deadline for withdrawal, authorizing mobilization of a massive multinational military force and using it to roll back Iraq's army of invasion. When warring factions seemed on the verge of genocide in Bosnia and when Somalia plunged toward anarchy, Security Council members eventually agreed on the importance of UN intervention. When Namibia moved toward independence, the UN helped. When Cambodia, Liberia, Haiti and nations in Central America held elections, the UN sought to assure fairness by supervising the voting process.

In other parts of the world, Rwanda for example, the UN failed to act with the decisiveness that could have prevented or minimized conflicts. In some cases, it stood on the sidelines while warring parties slaughtered the innocent. Nonetheless, post–Cold War UN actions demonstrate that cooperation among Security Council members can be achieved and that, even as it presently is constituted, it is far from impotent. Despite its checkered record and inherent limitations, I am convinced it can succeed in the enforcement of antiaggression, antiweapons law.

I must confess that I did not always feel this way. As long as the world was polarized by superpower rivalry, I saw no hope that the Security Council could carry out its responsibility to enforce a worldwide reign of peace. I felt it was necessary for the international community to create a new enforcement agency that would be independent of the UN and free of the system that has handcuffed the Security Council during much of its existence. I could not believe that the tradition of superpower rivalry could be overcome or that Security Council members could reach agreement on urgent matters of global importance.

My mind started to change in 1990 when Security Council members joined in condemning Iraq's aggression against Kuwait. I was struck by the fact that Russia, an ally of the Iraqis, declined to exercise its veto. My respect for the Security Council started to revive and I was further encouraged when it attempted to deal with problems in Bosnia, Somalia, Liberia, Haiti, Angola and other locations. While I had doubts about some of the decisions and many of the details of UN involvement, I became convinced that a new enforcement agency would be redundant and impractical. With a few changes in structure and a new positive, cooperative attitude, the Security Council could do the job. It could be an effective force in ending aggression and preserving peace.

Eliminating or Bypassing the Veto

Obviously, serious attention must be given to the elimination of the veto. It is a major obstacle to the implementation of a global rule of law. It gives one nation the power to override the decision of a majority. It gives national interests ascendancy over international interests. It ignores the reality of today's interconnected, interdependent world. It accentuates the differences that may exist among nations rather than the mutuality of their interests. It confirms the sad fact that fear and distrust continue to dictate the thinking of policymakers in capitals around the world.

Getting rid of the veto will be a challenging, if not impossible, undertaking. The governments of the five permanent members of the Security Council will be under great domestic pressure to resist the forces of UN Charter reform. They will not easily give up authority that has been their nations' possession for more than five decades. They will not want to take any action that will be perceived as eroding national sovereignty.

But the veto is an option and nothing more. As a practical matter, all that is needed to eliminate it is what we used to call a gentleman's agreement. If the leaders of the five permanent powers will shake hands and renounce use of the veto, the playing field will be leveled and all nations will be assured that fair play is the rule for the future. Then the impossible will become possible. The forces of reform will triumph and the pernicious influence of the veto will disappear like so many other vestiges of a past and outmoded age.

In many ways, the veto already has been doomed by the unifying imperative that created the European Union, the North American Free Trade Zone and the World Trade Organization. Eventually, the growing popular understanding that this is one world will make the Security Council into a truly effective instrument in the battle to save civilization from the threat of weapons of mass destruction.

Drawing Strength from Ratification

Unfortunately, reform will not come overnight. Abolition of the veto will take time when there is little time to spare. The possibility of nuclear blackmail or, as General Lee Butler put it, ". . . the nightmarish prospect of nuclear terror at the micro level" necessitates immediate action. So while every effort is made to replace the veto with a system that more nearly conforms with democratic principles, the Security Council must get on with its work. It must, to the best of its ability, assume responsibility for the enforcement of the law that will save the world from destruction.

The UN Charter authorizes the Security Council to enforce international law. In addition, the ratification process that we discussed earlier requires that antiaggression, antiweapons law be endorsed by two-thirds of all nations, including those with the strongest economies. This requirement will give the Security Council unmistakable authority to act on behalf of civilized humanity. It also will send a related message. It will tell Security Council members that they have been presented with an immensely important responsibility that should not be contravened by narrow national interests.

Given the strength of the two-thirds ratification formula, Security Council members should understand that utilization of the veto is not in conformity with the thinking of the global community. The world does not want a continuation of obsolete concepts of national interest. It does want to do away with the game-playing of conventional diplomacy and the perilous one-upmanship of military posturing. It wants Security Council members to forget about the veto and start working in good faith to provide evenhanded, nonprovocative law enforcement.

Importance of Public Opinion

Are the members capable of meeting this challenge? Will they be willing to voluntarily change their ways? Will they be ready to think in the international terms that, in the long run, will be best for their own countries?

I believe the answer to these questions depends on the knowledge possessed by everyday citizens. Suppose, for example, that a majority of the people of the United States come to realize that weapons of mass murder constitute a danger that no longer can be tolerated by civilized society, that economic power can be used to enforce the elimination of these weapons and that obstacles to enforcement must be eliminated. When it is clear that such beliefs are held by most Americans, the U.S. government will do everything in its power to cripple or eliminate the veto option. Our leaders will do what the leaders of democratic nations often do. They will follow the dictates of public opinion.

Even in less democratic nations, public opinion plays a role in influencing governmental policies. In recent years, the size of this role has been dramatically increased by the explosive development of two-way, worldwide communications. Now even the most repressive regime cannot succeed in totally stemming the across-border flow of information and ideas. As a result, the reality of the present threat to our planet and the global nature of today's society cannot be kept from thoughtful people no matter where they live, how they are governed or what political opinions they hold. The truth will overcome the artificial barriers created by politicians and compel governments to act in behalf of civilized society.

In this age of the everyday citizen, those who are in step with the present and who want to do something about the future have an obligation to speak out. We have a solemn duty to spread the word about the dangers we face and about the opportunities that can flow from the establishment of a lawful world. If we become advocates rather than spectators, I am confident leaders around the world will hear our voices and act in the best interests of humanity. They will see to it that, with or without amending the UN Charter, the veto power no longer will cripple the enforcement capabilities of the Security Council.

We Need to Meet Our UN Financial Obligations

Our voices also can help in other ways to strengthen the Security Council. For one thing, we can insist that all nations pay their UN membership dues. The United States has been by far the biggest nonpayer. Members of Congress have held UN dues hostage to policy questions such as abortion. They have complained, perhaps with some justification, that the UN's bureaucracy is notoriously inefficient. But they also must understand that by withholding payments, the U.S. has contributed to the financial instability that tends to breed inefficiency. Still worse, by our refusal to promptly meet our financial obligations, we have been tacitly telling the world that we really do not attach great importance to the UN. By delaying our payments, the United States has been weakening an organization that we will need as we work to lead the world into a new age of harmony and cooperation. Despite its flaws and failings, the UN has great potential. It offers proof that nations can work together for the common good. It demonstrates that international agreement can be achieved and that at least some of the problems faced by humanity can be solved with cooperative effort and without confrontation.

Expanding Security Council Membership

Another area that I believe deserves our attention is Security Council membership. The five permanent member nations were the major victors of World War II. Since then, Germany and Japan have made a striking recovery from defeat. Germany has reassumed its role as a dominant force in Europe while Japan has become an economic power of enormous global importance. By any measure of strength and influence, these two nations have become major players in world affairs and the leadership of the Security Council would be enhanced if they were seated as permanent members. With seven permanent members representing key participants in the international economy and ten rotating members providing broader national and regional participation, the Council's law enforcement ability will be enhanced and the trust placed in it by the world community will be increased.

Trust is important. The world must understand that the Security Council cannot carry out its enforcement responsibility in a climate of doubt and suspicion. Nations need to realize that the Security Council cannot function effectively unless they have faith in its fairness. Nations—citizens and leaders alike—need to know that the Council will not be authorized to threaten the territory or people of any law-abiding nation. Instead, it will work to eliminate the aggressive capabilities of all nations. The goal will be a world in which nations are able to protect themselves but are not tempted to attack others. As President Roosevelt noted in a 1933 statement to the Geneva Disarmament Conference, "If all nations will agree wholly to eliminate from possession and use weapons which make possible a successful attack, defenses will automatically become impregnable, and the frontiers and independence of every nation will become secure."

Enforcement through Cooperation

Traditionally, the Security Council has drawn its peacekeepers from the military forces of UN members. It wisely has not attempted to build up a permanent armed international police agency. Such an agency would undermine trust. It would be viewed as a threat and neither the leaders nor the citizens of the world's nations are eager to replace old threats with new ones. Neither leaders nor citizens will want to exchange the potential danger posed by a neighbor for the potential danger posed by an international military establishment. Besides, it is inconsistent and counterproductive to use warlike means to eliminate war, a lesson we should have learned from "the war to end wars" of 1914 to 1918.

In the past, the Security Council's most notable law enforcement efforts have involved the dispatch of peacekeeping units to trouble spots in order to separate warring parties and protect civilian lives. If I had my way, the Security Council's future peacekeeping efforts will continue to rely heavily on regional defensive organizations like NATO to provide necessary troops and equipment. By developing close cooperative ties with regional alliances, the Security Council will be positioned to promptly detect and verify acts of aggression and to respond with minimum delay.

In the lawful world we have been discovering, the Security Council also will need a monitoring component in its enforcement mechanism. The Council not only will have to react to problems of aggression, it will have to prevent problems by making sure all nations are in compliance with the antiweapons part of the new, binding international law. To accomplish its monitoring mission, the Security Council will have to rely on the cooperation and technological expertise of UN members, especially the United States and the Russian Federation, the nations that have the most experience in the detection of forbidden weapons. Through photo reconnaissance, infrared sensors, radar and other techniques, they have been able to catalog and evaluate the weapons of mass destruction in the possession of each other and of additional real or potential rivals. They have weapons detection capability and they should be called on to assist the Security Council as it works to identify the nations or groups that threaten the peace and security of the world.

Under the INF and START treaties, American and Russian observers have gone beyond remote monitoring procedures. On-site observers have penetrated installations that once were top secret. They have shown that on-site inspection can be nonthreatening and useful. The importance of on-site inspections was further underscored in the aftermath of the Gulf War when inspectors operating under UN authority and over the the strong objections of Iraq uncovered undeniable evidence that the Iraqis were working on a massive program to build weapons that would have had a devastating effect on their neighbors.

Reducing the Threat of Aggression

With a regularized system of law and a reliable law enforcement mechanism in place, the ability of a Saddam Hussein or any other dictator to frustrate and humiliate the world community will be diminished. The world's nations no longer will have to address problems on a reactionary ad hoc basis. They will not have to beg or buy the support that assures enforcement of the law. They will have established a procedure that is broadly applicable, fair, nonviolent and clearly understood. A nation violating international law through aggression or through possession of illegal weapons can expect to be called to account before the Security Council.

The Council already has the power to impose and enforce economic sanctions against a nation that violates international law. These could involve a partial or complete prohibition of trade with the lawbreaking nation and with nations that persist in doing business with the lawbreaker. As we've seen, the sanctions would be targeted against the leadership elite of the lawbreakers, not against innocent civilians, and the Security Council could provide for the exemption of food and medicine. Once the enforcement procedure is established, there should be none of the uncertainty or delay that can encourage a renegade state to prolong its defiance of civilized authority.

Answering the Sovereignty Question

The work of implementing sanctions will fall to the UN member nations that possess the means of sealing the borders of a lawbreaker and, if necessary, its trading partners. If this land, sea and air blockade is promptly and consistently imposed, if there is no doubt that it has the resolute support of the world community, I am certain that it will halt aggression and take weapons of mass destruction out of the hands of criminal nations.

Of course, it can be argued that the Security Council's system of inspections, verification and enforcement will infringe on national sovereignty. But this question raises two others: Does national sovereignty include the right to incinerate innocent men, women and children? Does national sovereignty include the right to threaten the continuation of life on this planet? A family has the right to defend its home from hostile neighbors. It has no right to burn its neighbor's house to the ground and slaughter all of its inhabitants.

Reduced Risk of Catastrophe

An antiaggression, antiweapons law enforced by the Security Council offers a practical way to protect nations and their people. But practical as it is, the way will not be easy. The concept is too new, too unconventional to be accepted without question. Leaders and citizens from all around the world will have to be convinced that the Security Council can succeed in assuring compliance. They will have to be assured that cheating can be prevented, that aggression can be halted and that the terror of sinister weapons can be barred from the face of the earth. With law in place and its strict enforcement a fact of life, why would any nation run the risk of being a violator? Why would any nation jeopardize its economic future by trying to build or conceal an outlawed weapon?

Certainly no nation governed by rational individuals would challenge a law that clearly is in the best interests of all. No nation that perceives the law's many benefits would set about to undermine it. But rationality and perceptiveness are not always present in the leadership elite. Deranged and evil people have been in charge in the past and it is reasonable to suppose that others will be in charge in the future. Some of these well may attempt to violate the law by building or concealing a banned weapon. But if the Security Council lives up to its responsibilities, and I believe it will, the outlawed weapons will be detected and confiscated and appropriate economic punishment will be imposed.

If the forces of evil gain control of a nation, there always is a possibility of a violent reaction to a Security Council decision. The outlaw nation could use its illegal weapons in an insane attack against the authority of civilized society. The result would be a catastrophe of gigantic proportions. But the catastrophe would be limited. Death, injury and destruction would be beyond belief. But the casualties and damage would be infinitely less than we could expect in the world as it exists today. Under present conditions, a nuclear, biological or chemical attack by one nation could trigger a series of responses that could destroy much of the planet. The employment of illegal weapons by one nation could start a chain reaction of attack and counterattack that could bring civilization to its knees.

With world law and an established enforcement system, weapons of mass murder no longer will fill the arsenals of many of the world's nations. The danger of irrational or accidental attack will be diminished. The nation that in an act of madness or defiance violates the prohibition against these weapons—and I do not think there will be many—will be the ultimate loser. It will be subject to economic penalties of such severity that they will destroy the offender's economy and render it incapable of supporting aggressive behavior. Nonviolence will replace violence. The culture of war will be replaced by the culture of cooperation.

Of course, the global system of law and law enforcement that we have been identifying will not work to perfection. No product of humanity's intelligence and imagination ever does. But I believe it will work far better than anything that has been proposed or attempted in the past. Violations of the law will be the exception, not the rule. If there is a nuclear, biological or chemical attack—and I believe such an occurrence is extremely unlikely—it will involve only a few warheads or a few tanks of deadly gas, not thousands. The world will be wounded. But it will survive.

With the establishment of the rule of law on an international level and with the Security Council functioning as the law's enforcement agency, the persuasive force of economic power will be on the side of all who seek the Fourth Freedom.

CHAPTER THIRTEEN

Creating Courts that Count

When Kansas and Colorado have a quarrel over the water of the Arkansas River they don't call out the National Guard in each state and go to war over it. They bring suit in the Supreme Court of the United States and abide by the decision. There isn't a reason in the world why we can't do that internationally.

—Harry S Truman

Now that we've seen the necessity of world law and the wisdom of delegating its enforcement to the Security Council, we should have no trouble identifying the piece that's missing from the institutionalized plan for international security that we've been seeking. For the plan to work, it must include a court system.

Such a system will give fairness and balance to the plan. It will strengthen the global rule of law by providing an orderly way to settle disputes. It will offer the weak as well as the powerful an opportunity to be heard, decide the fate of those charged with criminal activity, safeguard human rights and restrain illegal activities.

As Americans, we understand the importance of the judicial branch of government. We know that an effective court system is essential to our freedom. We realize that without our courts and the trust we place in them, the United States would be far different, and far worse, than it is today.

I believe our experience with the court system provides a useful lesson for global society. When the world submits to the rule of law—as it surely will when it understands that its very survival is at stake—it also must agree to the creation of the judicial institution needed to interpret the law, resolve international disagreements and determine the guilt or innocence of national leaders charged with behavior that threatens world peace.

A Weak International Court of Justice

Fortunately, part of an international court system already is in place. The International Court of Justice was authorized in the United Nations Charter. It has its headquarters in the Hague and its fifteen judges are prepared to decide international arguments and to offer opinions to the Security Council.

But there is one problem: The Court's jurisdiction is not compulsory. Nations do not have to submit their disputes to the Court and, if they do, they do not have to abide by the Court's decision.

As you might expect under these conditions, not all nations have been willing to place their trust in the Court's wisdom and objectivity. Not all have volunteered to put aside their shortsighted and antiquated understanding of sovereignty. They have lacked the courage to risk the possibility that the Court might hand down a decision that was contrary to national policies or interests. As a result, truly controversial issues, the ones that are most likely to spark armed conflict, rarely are brought to the Court's attention. Actions that could lead to war are discussed in the Security Council, the General Assembly, the news media and on the Internet, but almost never in the International Court of Justice.

Since its creation in 1945, the Court has devoted most of its energies to defining international law as expressed in treaties and other international agreements. It also has settled some vexing border disputes involving smaller nations. But during the Cold War confrontation of superpowers, when questions of life and death were constantly being asked and answered, the Court spent much of its time on the sidelines, not the playing field. When circumstances did allow it to offer an opinion, the results were entirely predictable. For example, in the 1980s the Court found the United States violated international law by mining harbors in Nicaragua, an action designed to support anticommunist rebels. The U.S. not only ignored the decision but it declared that the Court had no jurisdiction.

Again, U.S. Leadership Is Essential

Of course, the United States is not the only country to have turned its back on the authority of the International Court of Justice. But as I have pointed out, the United States is not just another country. It has a special place in the world's councils of power. It is the leader. It has an unmistakable obligation to encourage the acceptance of the international rule of law and to embrace the institutions that apply the law to the conduct of nations. It has the influence to bring about the world community's unconditional acceptance of a court system that will assure the law's fair and impartial application. It has the leverage to help civilized humanity take a giant step forward in its pursuit of the justice that is the foundation of lasting peace.

From the earliest times, civilized people have submitted themselves to the rule of law. They have obeyed the decisions of those individuals empowered to render legal judgments. They have acknowledged the authority of the law and the courts. They have realized that the alternative to law and courts of law is lawlessness, anarchy and the disastrous dissolution of the institutions that maintain social order. In their roles as citizens, civilized people also have supported their leaders when, in rare moments of enlightenment, they turned to independent tribunals to settle differences among states. For centuries, civilized people have realized that court proceedings, prolonged and frustrating as they might be, are infinitely more desirable than military action.

Creating an Impotent International Court

Yet, the ad hoc courts created over the centuries to adjudicate disputes among states were as infrequent as they were powerless. With few exceptions, chieftains and kings, presidents and parliaments were not ready to concede the interdependence of society or the futility of war. They viewed national sovereignty as a divine right that could not be restricted by any outside authority. Then, to use a current expression, came a wake-up call: World War I. Before it was over, an estimated 1.6 million French soldiers were dead and so were 2.4 million Germans, 1 million from the United Kingdom, 950,000 from Italy, 2.9 million from Russia, 2.3 million from Austro-Hungary and 126,000 from the United States. The numbers, like the carnage they represent, are beyond belief. Still, they tell only part of the story. They do not include millions of civilian deaths, the permanent crippling wounds suffered by additional millions of soldiers and civilians or the incalculable cost associated with the destruction of homes, churches, schools, libraries, factories and other material resources.

As they looked over the rows of white crosses and the blackened, smoking debris, the world's leaders and the citizens they were supposed to represent could not have helped but conclude something was terribly wrong with the organization of international affairs. How could so many supposedly brilliant people so totally miscalculate the scope of the danger? Why had so few understood what was at stake? Why had they allowed an act of terrorism, as regrettable and repugnant as it was, to trigger a war that would scar the landscape and the human soul for a generation? Why had they been willing participants in an escalation of threats that resulted in the most savage and destructive conflict in human history and set the stage for a second world war of even graver consequences?

Of course, they could not have predicted that the pistol shots fired at Archduke Francis Ferdinand in Sarajevo would reverberate for three decades, that the sound would grow in volume and intensity until it reached a deadly crescendo over Hiroshima. They could not have foreseen the technological advancements that have put awesome destructive power into the hands of terrorist gangs or the speed with which the devastating forces of war would threaten to engulf the cities and neighborhoods of the world. They could not have predicted that the final years of the twentieth century would be the most perilous in human history.

Indeed, when the leaders of the major powers sought to tie up the loose ends of international affairs at the end of World War I, they projected an image of hopefulness. They had redrawn the map of Europe, reduced the power of Germany, altered the configuration of colonial territories and created the League of Nations. Then they added a final touch to their plan for peace by establishing the Permanent Court of International Justice. This new court reflected a growing understanding of the importance of international law. Its establishment demonstrated that the world's leaders were coming to the realization that war was intolerable and that the only way to prevent it was through enforcement of the laws of civilized behavior.

For a time, it seemed that the world had come to its senses, that mechanisms to effectively prevent armed conflict were now in place, that the League and the Court were prepared to enable nations to settle their disputes through arbitration and litigation and not through artillery bombardments and bayonet charges. The world seemed poised for a new period characterized by what politicians in many nations undoubtedly referred to as "peace and progress." The dream of generations seemed close to fulfillment and people in all walks of life appeared to have good reason to demonstrate renewed confidence in the future.

Sadly, the bright hopes of the post–World War I years soon faded. The League proved itself to be the ultimate toothless tiger. Powerful nations gave it, at best, lip service while the United States, a nation that took justifiable pride in its moral leadership, did not even become a League member. The Permanent Court of International Justice, like its successor, the International Court of Justice, lacked mandatory jurisdiction. The creators of this "permanent" institution guaranteed its impermanence by making obedience to its authority voluntary rather than compulsory.

Mandatory Courts Are a Necessity

Clearly, the world's most recent attempts to build a structure for peace on the wreckage of war have been disappointing. In a span of less than three decades, world leaders created two world courts that could accurately be described as impotent. I would like to think that those who bear responsibility for the ineffectiveness of the courts acted with the best of intentions. But as my father often reminded me, "The road to hell is paved with good intentions."

Good intentions do not make good policy. What the world needed in 1921 and again in 1945, was a giant dose of realism. It needed to realize that a court without mandatory authority is certain to fail. A court that depends on voluntary participation has not the slightest chance of influencing the relationships of nations.

But as my family and friends well know, I am a devout optimist. I continue to believe we can learn from the mistakes of those who went before us. We can put the lessons of history to work on the salvation of our future. In every country on the face of the earth there are men and women of goodwill. I believe these individuals, most of them common individuals, can overcome doubts and distrust. I believe they can bridge the barriers that separate people and induce the leadership of their nations to take constructive action. They can play a pivotal role in turning the Security Council into an effective law enforcement agency and they can make sure the world has a court system that will provide the evenhanded application of international law that is essential in building a climate of productive cooperation.

The starting point for the establishment of such a court system is the reform of the existing world tribunal. The International Court of Justice must cease to be a cafeteria where each nation can pick and choose the legal arrangements that best suit its narrow national purposes. It must become a full-service restaurant where all nations are entitled to receive generous portions of justice. The Court must have mandatory jurisdiction and its rulings must be binding on all nations without exception or reservation.

Guideposts for an International Court

The details I will leave to the lawyers who, as I understand it, are available in plentiful numbers in the United States and perhaps some other parts of the world. However, before the lawyers have their say, let me state a few general principles. I believe any nation—rich or poor, powerful or weak—must have the right to bring its grievances before the Court. There it must be given a full hearing conducted in the most objective and thorough manner by jurists who are competent, impartial and incorruptible. The hearing must be open to the public and to representatives of the mass media. Both plaintiff and defendant must have the right to be represented by capable legal counsel. Most important of all, judgments of the Court must be accepted not only by all litigants but by all the nations of the world.

The scope of the Court's authority will be broad. Nations will be encouraged to bring their grievances and problems to the Court's attention. The United Nations will seek the Court's assistance in a variety of matters. It will be asked to decide the legitimacy of international institutions and agreements, to offer advisory opinions on important issues, to rule on what does or does not constitute a violation of international law. I expect that the Court also will hear appeals from rulings by the Security Council and objections to resolutions passed by the General Assembly.

The Court also will be asked to rule on trade matters and on issues involving multinational corporations. When its power is recognized in the world community, the Court will be a busy place, a global justice center that attracts all those who seek fairness in resolving their differences. However, if I had my way, I would make sure the Court does not get bogged down answering trivial, legalistic questions. I would insist that it give priority to questions of war and peace, the questions that constitute the fundamental reason for the Court's existence.

As I see it, the newly reformed International Court of Justice will bear a strong resemblance to the United States Supreme Court. Like the U.S. Supreme Court, the International Court of Justice will have paramount judicial authority. It will be the judicial arm of a global system specifically designed to keep us from destroying ourselves. It will review and judge the decisions and operations of the administrative and legislative arms. It will give international law strength and power. It will be the court of last resort for those who look for peaceful solutions to the problems that divide the nations of the world.

To enforce its opinions, the Court will rely on the Security Council. The Council, in turn, will utilize the carrots and sticks, the incentives and sanctions of economic power. If necessary, the Council can escalate its disciplinary actions by imposing total economic isolation on a nation that flouts a Court ruling. The Council will have the authority to authorize the establishment of a land-sea-air blockade, a sealing of borders that, at the very least, will gain the attention of the offending nation and remind all nations that the days of voluntary compliance with the rules of civilized behavior are gone forever.

Primary Responsibility: International Security

Unlike the U.S. Supreme Court which can review the decisions of state courts, the International Court of Justice should not be empowered to accept appeals from the decisions of national courts or of regional courts such as those now functioning in the European Union. The only exception would be when a ruling by a national or regional court constitutes a clear threat to world peace. Perhaps at some time in the future, the International Court of Justice should have broad, worldwide appellate jurisdiction. However, at this moment in history I think it would be wise to allow the Court to focus attention on its primary responsibility of enhancing international security. Turning the Court into a tribunal for appeals from national or regional courts would be a major distraction. It would dramatically multiply the number of pending cases, creating a backlog that would slow the pace of justice and eventually require the expansion of the Court and its bureaucracy.

Giving the Court routine appellate jurisdiction over national and regional courts would be, in my view, politically undesirable. It would unnecessarily open old wounds relating to traditional, and now fading, notions of sovereignty. For example, if the Court overturned a national court decision on educational standards, the decision could be a source of international division rather than harmony. It could be seen as meddling in a matter that is primarily of national concern. It could contribute to distrust of the Court and of all international institutions, including those essential to the preservation of peace.

Besides, the Court will have more than enough challenges to overcome. It will have to decide cases involving many of the root causes of conflict. It will have to answer complex questions that often are tied to economic realities, perceptions of historic events and cultural differences. It will have to reconcile divergent views of human rights and, when one right appears to be in conflict with another, it will have to develop a position that resolves arguments without sacrificing fundamental principles. A tall order? Yes, but if you agree with me that the rule of law is our only hope for the future, it is an order well worth placing and filling. If we have faith in the law, then we must also have faith in the ability of a world court of law to produce the answers required by a civilized society.

Self-Defense versus Self-Determination

Let me cite just one of the questions that faces society and an international court created to do society's work. From the earliest times, humanity has believed in the right of self-defense. People have the right to defend themselves and their property. Nations have the right to defend themselves against aggression. From time to time, this right has been qualified by church and civil authority. For example, defensive measures must be proportional to the danger. If your life has not been threatened, your right of self-defense does not extend to taking the life of another. You cannot defend your wallet by shooting and killing a pickpocket. But even with such qualifications and limitations, the right of self-defense is universally accepted and exercised. Indeed, even aggressors customarily claim their actions are motivated by their desire to defend themselves.

The Court will be called on to decide the legitimacy of claims of self-defense and the issue will become even more complex when the right of self-defense clashes with the right of self-determination. Again from the earliest times, groups of people have struggled to avoid domination by others. The Irish have resisted control by the British. Palestinians seek to gain authority over the areas they occupy in Israel. The Kurds have sought to establish a nation independent of Turkey, Iraq and other states. The Chechens have aggressively pursued their goal of autonomy from Russia. The Tamil minority wants independence in Sri Lanka. Zulus, Hutus, Tutsis and other African ethnic groups desire to be free to enjoy at least a degree of self-government. In the former Yugoslavia, a textbook example of the problem of conflicting rights, the desire for self-determination, for ethnic separation, has led to death, destruction and dislocation on a massive scale, devastating the economy, mortgaging the future and delaying realization of the dream of Pax Europa. To some, the rebellious groups, the people fighting to confirm their own identities, are freedom fighters. To others, they are traitors pursuing a course that will lead to national disaster.

So which right prevails? Does Russia's right of self-defense take precedence over the Chechens' right of self-determination? Do the Irish, Kurds, Tamils and all the others have the right to use arms in defense of their ethnic interests? Can minority groups redraw national boundaries at gunpoint? Can a national government use military force to prevent a minority from achieving its goals? And how much force is legitimate? How much is proportionate to the danger posed by minority demands?

Dealing with the Problem of Civil War

These questions are of critical importance. In recent years, the principal threats to world order have come not from confrontations among the major powers but from civil wars in Asia, Africa, Latin America and Europe. While these conflicts rarely have triggered wider involvement by neighboring states, they have resulted in an appalling number of deaths through military action, famine and disease. As many as 90 percent of the casualties are noncombatants and those who are fortunate enough to survive face a future of continuing fear and suffering.

In the past, the world has done little to respond to the horrors that bubble up from political, ethnic and religious rivalries within national borders. There are too many questions about rights that are in apparent conflict, too much uncertainty about authority, too much indecision about the responsibilities of national governments and international agencies. Without a court system empowered to deal effectively with life and death issues, the world community has chosen to turn its back to civil strife that victimizes individuals and tears the fabric of global peace and cooperation.

With a reformed International Court of Justice and its compulsory jurisdiction, the world at last will have a mechanism for dealing with the outrages committed in the name of national self-defense or group self-determination. It will have a tribunal empowered to examine the issues and produce opinions that are binding on all parties. It will have the authority to order governments to comply with decisions that reflect the consent of the world community.

Punishing National Leaders for Criminal Acts

Of course, governments are composed of people and, when a government is found guilty of violating international law, it may be necessary to bring the leaders of that government before the bar of justice. The

Hitlers, Stalins, Saddam Husseins and Slobodan Milosevics of today and tomorrow must be charged with their crimes and tried in a court of law. If they are found guilty, they must be sentenced to a punishment that reflects the evil they have done to their own people, the people of neighboring states and the security of the world. To handle this task, the world needs an International Criminal Court with compulsory jurisdiction over matters involving the peace-threatening actions of national leaders.

There is precedent for such a court. After World War II, the United States, Britain, the Soviet Union and France established an International Military Tribunal that convened in Nuremberg and passed judgment on German leaders charged with responsibility for initiating the war, violating norms for the conduct of war and committing "crimes against humanity." The latter category included genocidal and inhumane actions against minorities and the political opposition. A similar tribunal was convened in Tokyo to hear charges against Japanese military and civilian leaders.

The Nuremberg and Tokyo trials were celebrated for their trailblazing effort to enforce standards of civilized behavior. They also were criticized as an effort by the victors to punish the vanquished and some of the critics worried that the trials would set a precedent that could be applied to our own military leaders at the end of some future, unsuccessful conflict. U.S. Senator Robert A. Taft in a 1946 speech declared that the war crimes trials ". . . violate that fundamental principle of American law that a man cannot be tried under an ex post facto statute." While he may have been technically correct about the legal foundation of some of the charges, his overall argument was rejected in the court of public opinion. People around the world were appalled by the Nazi attempt to exterminate the Jews. They knew it was evil and they applauded the allied effort to bring the obviously guilty to justice.

In the 1990s, the Security Council created an international tribunal with the specific responsibility of bringing to justice those involved in mass murders, rapes and other crimes in the former Yugoslavia and Rwanda. Then the United Nations moved forward with the institutionalization of these tribunals and the creation of a permanent International Criminal Court.

As I noted earlier, the United States, in a shameful act of selfishness, led the fight against the permanent court. Spokesmen for our government objected to the independence proposed for the new court. They argued in favor of a criminal court that would be an arm of the Security Council and thus would be subject to the tyranny of the veto. In other words, the United States supported a criminal court but only if its power was severely restricted by vetoes or the threat of vetoes. Apparently, our leaders wanted a get-out-of-jail-free card that they could hand to the judge if some day they or their successors were called before the bar of international justice.

Fortunately, only a handful of nations stood with us in opposition to the permanent International Criminal Court and the final vote of 120 in favor to six against was one of the most total and shocking rejections of a U.S. position in the history of diplomacy. Those who stood in opposition to the United States recognized that ad hoc courts for specific crises are not an adequate response to the problem of international criminality. A permanent and independent criminal court is necessary to establish an effective system of enforceable international law.

With the International Criminal Court, there should be no such controversy. The court will not be a temporary addition to the system of justice. Its jurisdiction will be known and accepted by a clear majority of the world's nations. The laws it will enforce—primarily those banning aggression, weapons of mass destruction, state sponsored terrorism and the many mutations of genocide—also will be known and understood because ultimately they will have been endorsed through a public process involving all nations.

Making the Charges Clear

When the Security Council hands down what amounts to an indictment of a national leader who has violated international law, the reasons should be apparent to the nation's citizens and to people around the world. The Security Council will make public the charges and the evidence. It will call on the world community to assist in the apprehension of the defendant by supporting the Council's judicious use of economic sanctions.

Unlike the situation in the former Yugoslavia where leaders charged with ordering mass murder were allowed to remain at liberty for a prolonged period, the Security Council of the future must act decisively. If necessary, it must ask member nations or regional security organizations to take police action to bring the accused before the bar of justice. When a verdict has been reached, the International Criminal Court will make a special effort to communicate the reasons for its decision to the world. By explaining what it has done and why, the Court will be building public acceptance of the ruling and of the court itself.

Like the International Court of Justice, the International Criminal Court's judges will measure up to high standards of judicial performance. The judges will come from many nations and they will be elected for limited terms, perhaps by the Security Council and the General Assembly. Their main concern will not be retribution, revenge or compensation for victims but justice for humanity.

If defendants are found guilty of peace-threatening actions, the International Criminal Court will impose appropriate punishment that will be carried out by the Security Council. In my view, punishment must not exceed life imprisonment. While I concede that a Hitler or a Stalin—leaders who clearly were responsible for the deaths of millions—deserved the death penalty, there is a practical reason why this punishment must not be available to the International Criminal Court. To sentence a national leader to death is to create a martyr who will be a source of problems for generations. To execute a national or ethnic hero is to assure the hero's canonization or deification. In the minds of members of his or her group, the executed hero becomes a saint or a god who will be a rallying point for additional years of upheaval and adventurism.

Importance of Communication

When a leader is brought before the Court, both the Court and the Security Council must make an intense effort to communicate with the citizens of the leader's nation. They must be told the nature of the charges and the supporting evidence. They must be given a chance to follow the court proceedings by television or other means. Every effort must be made to show that the trial is fair and that the world community is justified in protecting itself from leaders who foment armed conflict by breaking the law against aggression or by possessing weapons of mass destruction.

The Court must be sensitive to religious, ethnic and cultural concerns. It needs to make a special effort to be perceived as an institution that serves the law with integrity and faithfulness. Its goal should be to earn a reputation as an independent, evenhanded dispenser of justice. People should come to think of the Court as what it is, an institution of great importance, one that has been charged by the community of nations with responsibility for upholding the law that protects civilized society.

When this happens, when the international court system is universally respected for excellence and objectivity, the world will be closer to realizing the dream we have been pursuing.

CHAPTER FOURTEEN

Summarizing Our Discoveries

I know of no way of judging the future but by the past.

—Patrick Henry

During our journey of discovery, we've toured many of the landmark events that helped determine the direction taken by America and the world since the end of World War II. Starting with the 1945 creation of the United Nations Organization, continuing through the Cold War and on to the decade of the 1990s with its nuclear testing by India and Pakistan and its conflicts in Yugoslavia, we've seen success and failure, encouragement and disappointment.

Most of all, we've witnessed the beginning of a transformation in the thinking of concerned individuals in many countries in every part of the globe. We've seen people and some of their leaders begin to look beyond violence to solve international security problems. The change has been gradual, almost imperceptible. But it is real and it offers renewed hope that during the twenty-first century humanity will not repeat the errors that brought unprecedented bloodshed and destruction to the twentieth century.

The UN: Playing an Essential Role

The UN itself is a monument to growing international concern about the future. Roosevelt, Churchill and other world leaders were determined that the horrifying carnage of the war must not be repeated. They created an organization designed to temper the destructive impulses of international competition and provide a forum for resolving disputes before they disintegrate into armed conflict. Their creation is far from perfect. But even with its many flaws, the UN has become an essential element in world affairs. It has fostered international cooperation and demonstrated that nations working together can achieve far more than a single nation operating on its own.

The UN also has shown that greater international cooperation does not mean world government. A stronger system of global agreement is not a threat to the independence and basic sovereignty of any nation, including the United States. Indeed, global cooperation is the best possible way of solving international disputes, dampening violence and assuring the rights of civilized society.

A Record of Progress

From the vantage point of history, we can see many signs of progress in civilization's continuing struggle to protect itself from the scourge of war. Through the Marshall Plan in Europe and similar enlightened policies in Japan, the United States revitalized its defeated enemies and set them on a course that led away from dictatorship and armed conflict and toward democracy and economic growth. The success of the Marshall Plan made a major contribution to the eventual triumph of democratic capitalism, the destruction of the Soviet Union and the end of the Cold War. Clearly, economic power was achieving goals that are beyond the reach of military action. International cooperation was demonstrating its worth in a variety of situations and the cause of civilized conduct was making progress in many regions of the world.

Peacekeeping efforts, though sporadic and inconsistent, lessened violence and sometimes moved opponents toward a peaceful resolution of their differences. In the Persian Gulf region, civilized nations united to resist an aggressor and to impose a trade embargo that kept a tyrant in his cage. And even though the tyrant escaped prompt punishment for his violation of international law, he stands condemned in the eyes of civilized society and the necessity of bringing to justice those charged with crimes against humanity enjoys strong worldwide support.

In the half-century since World War II, nations have agreed to cooperate in the elimination of chemical and biological weapons, in attempting to reduce the proliferation of nuclear materials and technology and even in the downsizing of existing stockpiles of nuclear warheads and delivery systems. Given these forward steps, there was good reason to believe that the obsolescence of war had become an accepted fact and that weapons of mass destruction, while still a threat, were far less likely to be employed by any legitimate governing authority. The cause of disarmament seemed to have become less urgent and, as the century drifted into its final moments, complacency gained control over the thinking of many national leaders.

Then India and Pakistan signified the reality of their long-standing enmity by testing nuclear devices. In a matter of hours, thinking people around the world were confronted with the realization that the possibility of catastrophic war had not been eliminated. Their justifiable fear was intensified by devastating war in the Balkans, long the starting point for European conflict. The root causes of armed conflict may have been diminished but they have not been eradicated.

Assessing the Causes of Conflict

We know many of these causes. For example, cultures and societies which glorify war and violence are more likely to resort to such behavior. But this behavior is not built into the genetic code. It is learned and it can be unlearned or modified. Children who watch violence on television are more likely to be violent than those who have not had this exposure. The remedy is obvious, simple and effective: reduce violence on television or keep children from viewing violent shows. But how can such a remedy be applied to a culture? How can a society be taught that violence is self-defeating, that armed conflict plays into the hands of humanity's oldest enemies, death, injury and destruction?

Then there is power. Some national leaders believe the essence of governance is the pursuit of power, for themselves and for their nation. They mistakenly believe that their thirst for power can be satisfied by investing precious national resources in armaments. They promote extreme nationalism, attempt to intimidate their neighbors and accept war as a legitimate tool of national policy. Although the pages of history are littered with the wreckage of leaders whose pursuit of power led to personal and national disaster, the power-obsessed do not seem to know or care. They seek short-term glory and they will not be deterred by appeals based on common sense.

In a democratic society, such leaders are not likely to gain control and, even if they succeed in achieving high office, they most probably will be restrained by the electorate. In a totalitarian state, popular sentiment means nothing and the dictator in charge is free to follow a course of action that is reckless and self-destructive.

Fortunately, the number of dictatorships has been shrinking since the end of World War II, another reason for optimism about the future. But even if the last dictatorship disappears from the face of the earth, we cannot be certain that war will follow a similar pathway to oblivion. Popularly elected officials are not above manipulating ethnic or racial hatred. They can play on the fears of their people and become cheerleaders for military expansion. They can pursue power without adequate regard for the consequences or morality of their actions.

The Necessity of a Civilized Plan of Action

While civilized society has moved closer to renouncing war as a legitimate instrument of national policy, it has not succeeded in eliminating the root causes of war or in constructing an institutionalized war-suppression system. We are still at the mercy of the immoral individuals who are willing to use war or the threat of war for their own purposes. But there is no reason for us to forever remain in our present perilous situation. We have the knowledge and the power to make the present moment a watershed in history, an age in which humanity finally wins its battle for the Fourth Freedom.

In our search for this freedom, we've identified the fundamental elements in a system that has the power to lift from society the burden of war and the fear of weapons of mass destruction. For years, I've been referring to these elements by a collective name—the Civilized Defense Plan or CDP, a system based on the following eight principles:

1. **International security can only be achieved through law.**
   Without the rule of law, the Fourth Freedom is an impossible dream. To assure Freedom from Fear to all the world's people, the law must be binding and enforceable. It must forbid armed aggression, possession and use of weapons of mass destruction, state-sponsored terrorism, genocide and other crimes against humanity.
2. **No nation is above the law.**
   The primacy of the rule of law is essential. Whether it takes the form of treaties, agreements reached under the auspices of the United Nations or other transnational arrangements, the law must be obeyed by all nations, rich and poor, democratic and authoritarian. As the world's most powerful nation, the United States has a special obligation to set the highest standards of continuing compliance with the law.
3. **The law must have broad support.**
   To assure the law's acceptance and enforcement, it must be ratified by two-thirds of the world's nations, including those doing two-thirds of all trade in manufactured goods. This formula guarantees that the law has the support of a super majority of nations, including those with the economic muscle to assure enforcement.
4. **The power of trade must be the primary means of enforcement.**
   There is abundant evidence that military power is an inhumane, ineffective and often counterproductive enforcement option. On the other hand, economic power is effective, humane and constructive. Economic incentives and sanctions, the ability to give and to withhold, produce the desired results in every aspect of human relationships, including international affairs. Through an enforcement system based on economic power, law-abiding nations will be rewarded and law-breaking nations will be penalized. Military force will be used only as a last resort.
5. **Sanctions must target both criminals and their accomplices.**
   To defy a lawfully imposed sanctions regime is a criminal act and it must be treated accordingly. If economic sanctions are imposed on

one nation, they must be recognized and obeyed by all nations. Any nation flouting sanctions by continuing to trade with a lawbreaking nation is guilty of breaking international law and must be treated accordingly. By sanctioning criminals and their accessories in crime, the community of nations will make it impossible for criminals to evade economic punishment through open or clandestine trade with opportunistic neighbors or allies. Nations complying with the law and cooperating with its enforcement will be eligible for economic rewards, trade benefits and security assurances.

6. **The UN Security Council must be responsible for enforcement.**
The UN Charter gives the Security Council authority to promote peace and maintain international order. Through the agreement of the world community, the Security Council has a mandate to enforce the law. It is positioned to detect violations and assess their gravity, decide appropriate economic penalties and organize the imposition of those penalties through the cooperation of law-abiding nations and regional security alliances. Security Council-imposed sanctions will be consistently multinational and will be targeted as much as possible against the leaders of nations found in violation, not against innocent civilians.

7. **International courts must have mandatory jurisdiction.**
Courts are necessary to assure fairness in the interpretation and application of the law and they must have mandatory jurisdiction. All nations must accept the judgments of the courts and no nation shall have the power to annul or veto a court judgment. The international court system must include a criminal division empowered to weigh the evidence and render judgment in cases involving national leaders accused of crimes against humanity. Punishment of convicted individuals shall be limited to life imprisonment.

8. **The United States must play a leadership role.**
America's economic strength, political stability and history of idealism in international affairs have given it a unique opportunity to lead the world to authentic security. By forsaking narrow national interests for the interests of humanity, the United States can take advantage of the increasing interdependence of nations. It can influence them to join in creating a new age of international cooperation under the law.

What CDP Can Give Us

The benefits of a lawful world are beyond question. Resources, both intellectual and physical, no longer will be wasted in vain attempts to gain military superiority. The cycle of violence will be interrupted and men and women will be free to turn their attention to overcoming the age-old adversaries of mankind, to the conquest of poverty, hunger and disease. With the burden of armaments lifted and confidence in the future restored, we will have the power to grow in knowledge of ourselves and our universe, restore the environment, explore the heavens and unravel the mysteries of mind and body. We will make the twenty-first century the most productive and rewarding in human experience.

All this and more can be achieved if we give CDP a chance, if we use it as a pattern for a future of international security under the rule of law. Is CDP perfect? Of course not. But after years of study and discussion and hours of debate with objectors and skeptics, I continue to believe CDP offers a rational way to achieve the Fourth Freedom.

It does not pretend to answer every question nor does it claim to provide a magic formula for ending society's long and abhorrent tradition of violence. The tradition already has cost the lives of millions. It made the twentieth century the cruelest and most destructive in history. It has made the present period of history arguably more dangerous than any in the past.

Uprooting the Tradition of Violence

But no tradition is permanent. If the tradition of violence cannot be uprooted, it can, at least, be diminished by the faith, commitment, goodwill and leadership of everyday individuals in America and around the world. If we stand up for what we know is right, if we seize the power that now is available to us, we can renew the face of the earth. We can replace the rule of force with the force of law and create a society that is united in striving for goals that benefit all nations, all races, all people.

We do not need extraordinary intelligence, knowledge, wisdom or courage to join in this effort. We do need the determination to share our beliefs and our understanding with others. We need to increase our realization of the interdependence of today's world and, if we are Americans, to tell our fellow citizens about the role the United States must play in creating a new age of cooperative security. We need to communicate our strong belief in the rule of law and why it must be strengthened here at home and extended to all the world.

By taking these small steps, we can play a major role in shaping tomorrow. We can contribute to the momentum that is moving civilization upward.

We Need to Know the Truth

Of course, there are obstacles. For example, we need to know as much as possible about the world situation and the scope of the dangers we face. Unfortunately, our government does not recognize our right to this information and it rarely favors us with the unadulterated truth. A case in point is its disinclination to share what it knows about the proliferation of weapons of mass destruction. We have been kept in the dark about the worldwide availability of dangerous biological and chemical substances, the scope of the Soviet effort to develop more deadly biological agents, the ease with which toxic materials could be introduced into our urban areas and the urgency of developing systems that can provide at least a moderate degree of protection.

Instead of giving people full and accurate information, our government hides behind the claim that disclosure will jeopardize national security. Of course, there are secrets that ought to be protected. But at least some of the information withheld from the people of our country often seems to be available to the governments of other nations, friends and enemies alike. It is a safe bet that Russian officials know more about our weapons and our strategy than do most Americans. And if the Russians know, can we doubt that the information has reached Iraqis, Serbs and others who maintain ties with Russia?

More than fifty years after Hiroshima and Nagasaki, our government has not told us the whole truth about nuclear weapons and their lethal effect. We have been led to believe that our country could survive a nuclear attack, launch a retaliatory strike and achieve victory. To support this scenario, the number of deaths and the amount of destruction have been routinely underestimated in official reports. Stansfield Turner, retired admiral and former director of the U.S. Central Intelligence Agency, put it directly in an appendix to his book, *Caging the Nuclear Genie:* "The executive branch of our government has been negligent, even irresponsible, in underestimating the impact nuclear weapons would have."

Without access to the truth, people will make potentially dangerous mistakes. They will elect leaders who are a threat to society, men and women who entice the people with promises and pander to the greed of the selfish. Without truth, people will accept policies based on falsehood and endorse programs that provide instant gratification rather than enduring progress. If truth is ignored, the legacy of America cannot be passed on to future generations. Our nation will be destined to follow the other great nations that vanished from history's pages.

The most recent example is the Soviet Union. It was built on falsehood and protected by a wall of oppression. When truth percolated through the wall, the USSR disappeared from the map of the world.

Present Circumstances Demand Immediate Action

Now Americans are suffering from their own form of truth deprivation. It manifests itself in the indifference that seems to pervade our society. We wake up to the peril when we hear a Chinese official declare that his nation has nuclear-armed missiles capable of striking Los Angeles or when India and Pakistan take turns rattling the nuclear saber. But our concern tends to be transitory. Without the information that would allow us to put the latest threats into context, we are not inclined to take action ourselves or to demand action from our government.

But time is running out. We cannot indefinitely postpone the action needed to banish fear of war from our own minds and from the minds of our fellow human beings. We must not turn our backs on the danger that confronts us. We no longer can allow ourselves to be content with a foreign policy that reacts to events and that seems incapable of taking the long view on matters that are of vital importance to our generation and the generations we hope will follow us.

Instead of clinging to its present reactionary habits of behavior, our country must provide leadership in its dealings with the world community. Our leaders must be forthright in describing the perils that face civilization. They must be consistent in supporting policies that encourage cooperation and promote the rule of law in international affairs. They must end the hypocrisy that serves only to undermine America's moral authority.

Hypocrisy is a strong word. But how else can you describe America's insistence that it has a right to maintain a nuclear arsenal while nations like India and Pakistan do not? What other label would you put on America's willingness to sell weapons of aggression to others while denouncing similar sales by China, Russia and North Korea?

Time to Ask Some Hard Questions

America's success is so pervasive that it has lulled many of us into a false sense of security and superiority. We think we are safe from the world's threats and we believe we are so strong that we can solve any problem with our dollars or our armaments. We fail to see that success may be our greatest enemy. It has dulled our understanding of reality and kept us from seeing the moral and ethical dimensions of our policies. No wonder Benjamin Franklin has been quoted as saying, "For success I have no remedy."

Success can be deadly to individuals, organizations and nations. But, contrary to Dr. Franklin's opinion, there is a cure. It begins with an examination of conscience and it includes an earnest attempt to see the world through the eyes of our neighbors in other countries. Then we ought to ask ourselves some hard questions about our country and how it is perceived by these global neighbors.

What kind of world do we want, not just for ourselves, but for all the people who share this planet with us?

Are we so economically obsessed, so inconsiderate of the lives of others, so morally bankrupt that we need to sell offensive weapons of any kind to anybody?

We profess to practice democracy as a nation, but do we practice it in relation to other nations? Do we treat them with respect? Do we recognize their rights?

Do we realize that the only way the United States can lead the world is by devoting its power to the creation of a world ruled by law?

America must set an example for the world. It must regard international law as sacrosanct. It must do everything possible to strengthen the United Nations without jeopardizing its own national sovereignty. We are not in competition with the UN. If the UN does something with which we do not agree, we must have the tolerance, patience, foresight and energy to work from within, to convince other UN members of the correctness of our position. We must use our influence to create a lawful, prosperous and peaceful world.

Giving Priority to Defense

In pursuing this world, there is another question we need to ask ourselves: What would be the effect on the world if the United States just said "no" to the armaments race by refusing to make offensive weapons? Why are we unwilling to face the fact that our Department of Defense was more accurately described by its former name, the Department of War? Why don't we transform it into a true Department of Defense by focusing our energies on developing reliable systems of defense while abandoning all forms of offensive weaponry?

As I pointed out earlier in this book, it sometimes may appear difficult to differentiate offensive from defensive. But I suspect the difficulty may have more to do with our natural tendency to complicate things than it does with reality. Clearly, all weapons of mass destruction are by their very nature offensive. Some other weapons can be used for both offensive and defensive purposes. But even if arbitrary definitions have to be assigned, the boundary between offensive and defensive weapons can be established. Then United States must come down squarely on the side of defense.

In doing so, we must be careful to avoid a Maginot Line mentality. We must not lock into place the crazy idea that we can protect ourselves from all danger. We must be careful not to communicate the notion that we do not trust other nations. By signaling our lack of trust, we very likely will provoke acceleration of an arms race that has poisoned international relations for decades.

If we attempt to build a shield against incoming ballistic missiles—the so-called "Star Wars" defense—we will be undermining the Anti-

Ballistic Missile (ABM) Treaty, the foundation of all of our arms reduction treaties with Moscow. We also will be spending trillions of dollars on a system few believe will work with any degree of consistency. Even if the space-based system stops all ballistic missiles before they can hit their targets, it cannot protect American cities from low-flying aircraft or cruise missiles or from suitcase nuclear bombs that could easily be concealed, transported and detonated by our enemies. Instead of spending our resources on unproven and questionable Star Wars technology, we need to take the lead in investing in defensive systems that would diminish the value of offensive arms the world over.

Standing Up for What Is Right

If the United States were to become a true arsenal of defense, the course of warfare could be changed and the prospect of any nation committing aggression against another would be dramatically reduced. Wars of aggression would become a thing of the past. Nations, including the United States, would have a more secure defense at lower cost and with less risk. By adding its weight to the defensive side of the armaments ledger, the United States would earn the right to be identified as one of the great nations of history. It would demonstrate that it has the courage to live by the principles on which it was founded.

This is an exciting prospect. Perhaps for the first time in history a nation would be signifying its recognition and acceptance of the truth. It would be providing concrete evidence that the weapons of offensive war are a sign of weakness, not strength, and that a defense based on long-term moral considerations, rather than short-term expediency, is invulnerable.

With the United States standing up for what is right and rallying to the defense of less powerful nations, fear of war ultimately will vanish from the face of the earth. Distrust, hatred, destruction and mass murder will be replaced by trust, compassion, creativity and life. We will have the freedom and the power to cross the threshold of a new age of extraordinary achievement. We will be able to join men and women of goodwill in America and around the world in raising civilization to a level that is beyond our power of imagination.

CHAPTER FIFTEEN

Looking into the Future

There is a tide in the affairs of men,
Which, taken at the flood, leads on to fortune;
Omitted, all the voyage of their life
Is bound in shallows and miseries.
On such a full sea are we now afloat,
And we must take the current where it serves,
Or lose our ventures.

—William Shakespeare

At this very moment, we are afloat on such a tide.

Despite continuing eruptions of nonsensical, barbaric warfare, the immorality and incompetence of American foreign policy and daily worldwide demonstrations of humankind's addiction to selfishness, suspicion and hatred, the currents of history are flowing in our favor. They are pushing civilized society toward an age of unprecedented cooperation and accomplishment, creating the levers that will enable people of goodwill to break the cycle of violence and free the world from fear.

The evidence is clear. Nations have begun to understand the necessity of working together. International trade is increasing at rates that were unthinkable a few years ago. A network of electronic connections has globalized the economy and homogenized many of the world's industrial, commercial, educational and cultural activities and resources. The one-world dream is well on its way to becoming reality.

More and more people are coming to recognize the reality of international interdependence. Many of them, in America and around the world, are questioning the reasoning that initiated and sustained the nuclear peril. They are beginning to see the folly of all weapons of mass murder. They are speaking out in favor of nuclear abolition and against terrorism, genocide and other crimes against humanity. The limitations, wastefulness, futility and counterproductive nature of military action is increasingly clear to millions of individuals. Faith in the future is inspiring everyday people in every country to step forward in support of freedom, democracy, security and justice.

Beyond question, we are entering an age in which the possibilities for responsible progress are so diverse and numerous that they overwhelm our power of imagination. A confluence of trends, innovations and developments has granted this generation and the one that will follow an opportunity that is as singular as it is important. It has given us a chance to make the present a turning point in history, to begin an age in which humanity finally wins its struggle against the evil of violence and achieves the Fourth Freedom.

As we know from our search, the key that will free us from fear of armed aggression, weapons of annihilation and many of the other horrors that continue to confront civilization is international law backed by an ethical, permanent, humane and institutionalized system of enforcement.

A Moral Code Governs the Universe

The world is too dangerous for us to indefinitely tolerate ad hoc diplomacy, knee-jerk reactions to security threats or military adventurism under the pretext of self-defense. The time is past due for the world to reject unilateral solutions to life-or-death international problems and to adopt a multilateral approach that is impartial in spirit and global in scope. This approach must be rooted in the belief that the universe in which we exist is governed by a moral code. We may not be able to comprehend all the workings of this code but without it, the order we see all around us would be replaced by chaos.

Life has taught me that achieving order is a primary, if unconscious, goal of all creation. From the galaxies of deep space to the relationships of societies, families and individuals, order is a necessity and, over the long haul, it is maintained by laws that are as compelling and balanced as they are immutable and eternal. Whether we realize it or not, adherence to the rule of law is essential for human survival. For the short term, individuals may violate the law and appear to get away with it. Men and women, including the highest officials of government, may act as if they are above the law and escape punishment. But in the grand scheme of universal justice, there is no lasting escape and every transgressor ultimately will pay a price.

Prospering under the Rule of Law

Law is an equalizer and a unifier. It establishes standards to which all can aspire. It makes us more productive and responsible. It is the hallmark of the civilized societies that have benefited us beyond measure. By observing how the rule of law has influenced and elevated human conduct through the ages, we not only increase our understanding of the past but we begin to see what must be done to assure humanity's future.

The future is far more than an extension of the present. It is a gift that we can accept or reject. It is a mystery that is both enormously attractive and profoundly frightening. The future is always just beyond reach, always challenging us to employ intellect and imagination to know its unknowable contours, always beckoning us to explore its reality and tempting us to expend our energy on penetrating the mists that obscure the days ahead.

A Book about the Future

In many ways, all of this book is about the future. In chapter after chapter, it lays out a plan to assure that ignorance, miscalculation or criminal behavior will not prevent the future from unfolding. If readers accept the plan, or at least the fundamental concepts on which it is based, they will have taken a first step toward ending the present state of denial and raising the curtain on a future of greatness.

For some time now, most of the earth's people have closed their minds to the danger posed by weapons of mass destruction, especially the thousands of nuclear devices that now are poised to obliterate life. The danger is real and immediate but millions choose to ignore it. Instead of confronting the very real possibility of Armageddon, they rely on national leaders who repeatedly have demonstrated an allergy to the truth. They prefer to hold tight to the comforting but mistaken belief that the end of the Cold War eliminated or, at least, greatly reduced the threat to survival that is inherent in the world's bulging nuclear arsenals.

Dangers of Denial

This denial of danger is unhealthy in the extreme. By closing their minds to the truth, people are slamming the door on tomorrow. They are condemning themselves and their families, friends and neighbors to annihilation. They are guaranteeing a catastrophic disaster that will mark the end of human history.

Perhaps I am inordinately naive, but I cannot bring myself to believe most people will be forever content to live the lie that repeatedly has been told to us by our national security establishment. I have unshakable faith in the wisdom of everyday people in my country and around the world. Once they realize the truth, they will take action to end the nuclear peril. By rejecting false notions of security, they will assure that the record of humanity's progress, a story that dates back thousands of years, will not end. More chapters will be written, more goals accomplished, more ground gained in humanity's effort to realize its potential.

A Consensus for Survival

When everyday people look the present danger squarely in the eye, they will waste no time in forcing their leaders to do the same. Then humanity will be moving toward a consensus for survival, an awareness that nuclear and other weapons of mass murder are inherently evil. People will come to understand that these weapons are not armaments in any traditional sense. They are the instruments of global suicide. Once people accept this truth, they will see to it that weapons of annihilation are totally and permanently banished. They will not tolerate the possession of annihilating devices by any nation or group of nations.

I cannot predict exactly when or how this will happen, but I am entirely confident that it will. I am equally confident that the abolition of weapons of mass murder will be accompanied by other positive developments. People will accept the necessity and inevitability of international law. They will see that the law is the guarantor of a Fourth Freedom that is global and enduring. They may even be open to the possibility that the law created to govern relationships among nations will reflect the universal law instituted at the moment of creation and perpetuated through the ages by a power that we cannot hope to know.

A New Golden Age

Under the rule of law, people of all nations will prosper in a climate of confidence and cooperation. They will move far beyond the present threshold of knowledge, learning how to manipulate the forces of nature, conquer hunger and disease, minimize human conflict, foster virtue and strengthen harmony at every level of society. Under the shield of law, the people of the future will penetrate the fundamental elements of the universe, expose the mysteries of the smallest particles of matter and energy and expand their knowledge of themselves and their neighbors.

Science will enter a new golden age and the arts will blossom in every region and every nation. Best of all, the lawful world of the future will be a place of spiritual renewal where the blessings of faith, hope and love will be as appreciated as they are abundant.

Repeated Errors by Our Leaders

Unfortunately, history teaches that the establishment of the lawful world of the Fourth Freedom will be neither easy nor automatic. In our own time, we have seen our leaders repeatedly ignore reality and turn their backs on common sense. They have persisted in overestimating the effectiveness of military force and underestimating the potential of economic power. Though they may have been acting with the best of intentions, they frequently have achieved results that are not in the national interest and that lessen the security of all nations and all people.

They have blundered into conflicts, unleashed deadly and pointless assaults, attempted to dictate the behavior of other nations and ignored our own obligations to the world community. Worst of all, our leaders have refused to admit their mistakes. When they find themselves mired in quicksand, they make no effort to extricate themselves. Instead, they plunge ahead, pulling the nation and the world closer to bottomless disaster.

In instance after instance, our leaders repeat their errors of judgment. They appear not to have learned anything from the Vietnam experience. They seem oblivious to the sea change in international affairs that accompanied the disintegration of the Soviet Union and the end of the Cold War. How else do you explain the maintenance of American armed forces in a Europe that no longer is threatened by the Soviet menace? Why is it that our leaders give such low priority to resolving hostilities on the Korean Peninsula where thousands of American troops stand guard as they have for nearly a half-century?

When an aerial assault against Iraq failed to topple its dictator and mainly succeeded in evicting international arms inspectors from the country, our leaders offered no admission of miscalculation. Instead, they launched additional missiles, destroying a medicine factory in Sudan and enhancing the status of a terrorist in Afghanistan. Then they picked up the NATO flag and began an action against Serbia that exacerbated the suffering of the Albanian minority in Kosovo and inflicted destruction for which we will be footing the bill for years to come.

Why do our leaders appear to be blind to the existence of nonviolent alternatives to military action? They are prepared to pay for the damage done by our military. Why are they unprepared to use our economic resources as an incentive that will move other nations away from hostility and toward reconciliation?

Why Have We Neglected Economic Power?

As we know from personal and career experience, money makes things happen. The threat of its withdrawal and the promise of its availability work wonders in convincing people to at least consider a change in attitude or an improvement in performance. Economic power conditions our thought processes and plays a major role in shaping our decisions. On the international level, it can be a powerful tool of diplomacy. It can provide a quantifiable and tangible reason for leaders to adopt a course of action that contributes to the progress and security of the nations they govern.

Why has the United States—by every standard of measurement the most powerful economic engine in history—been so reluctant to make economic power the cornerstone of its dealings with others? Why have we frittered away our economic strength on a military institution that repeatedly falls short when it comes to achieving our foreign policy goals? Why do we waste our resources on weapons so sinister that we will never agree to their use?

I cannot answer these questions, perhaps because no valid answers exist. But I know in my heart that asking is far from a waste of time. As more and more people come to question the wisdom of American policy, our leaders will hear the doubts and respond to them. In a democracy such as ours, the voice of the people is important. Sooner or later—and I believe it will be sooner rather than later—they will demand the rethinking of our foreign policy. Then America's leaders will begin to understand the necessity of using our economic influence to move humanity toward the rule of law.

Be Prepared for Failures and Setbacks

The effort to create a lawful world, to climb to a higher level of existence, certainly will be a struggle. We must expect many stumbles and we must be prepared for many failures and setbacks. Human nature will not be transformed overnight. We will not instantly shed jealousy, distrust and hatred. Religious and ethnic differences will not be immediately bridged, overcome or forgotten. We will not be able to say a quick goodbye to the violent tendencies that through the centuries have brought to the world a fearful harvest of pain, suffering and death.

The very existence of these tendencies is a powerful argument for the establishment of the rule of law. Only when the rule is in place globally will humanity be equipped to restrain the evil actions of evil doers, including those in positions of authority. The law will require lawful behavior by dictators as well as those elected through the democratic process. It will demand conduct that contributes to international cooperation.

An Element of Risk

In due time, the necessity of mandatory, global legal authority is certain to be understood by a clear majority of the world's people and they will insist on its implementation. But even with broad public support, the establishment of a legal system that meets the test of fairness and universality will not be free of risk. Even the essential step of abolishing nuclear weapons and institutionalizing their abolition through international law could have dire consequences. Through misunderstanding, incompetence or malevolence, humanity's attempt to alter the deadly status quo could result in a nuclear accident or attack that could kill thousands, destroy an urban area and create long-term social, economic and environmental disruption.

Nonetheless, if humanity wills the end of the nuclear nightmare, I have no doubt about the eventual outcome. Right will overcome wrong. The will of informed, dedicated men and women will triumph over all the dark forces that for decades have kept us and our children locked behind a wall of fear.

How can I be so certain? Because when we stop denying the danger, when we face up to the problem, when we decide to end our cohabitation with evil, the world will be changed forever. The illogical, unworkable and terrifying strategy of mutually assured destruction will be rejected. Instead of the massive strikes and counterstrikes presently contemplated by the nuclear warriors of the United States and other nations, the nuclear danger in a world under law will be limited in scope.

If there is an accidental nuclear explosion or even an attack executed by a terrorist, there will be no automatic deadly response, no escalation of hostilities, no threat of worldwide nuclear conflict. Creation will suffer and humanity will be punished for its ambitions and miscalculations. But coming generations will survive. They will have undergone, quite literally, a trial by fire and they will emerge with a new appreciation of humanity's fragility and a new understanding of what will be required of them to repress savagery and strengthen the cause of civilization.

A Horrifying Wake-Up Call

The detonation of a nuclear device, by accident or command, would be the ultimate call to action. It would shatter nuclear denial and provide the world with an unanswerable argument for nuclear abolition. It also would provide compelling evidence of the obsolescence of military force in the settlement of international differences. It would demonstrate that the military option is not an option at all. It is a counterproductive assault on life itself.

I pray that humanity will not require such a horrifying wake-up call. I believe the truth about military force and the preeminence of economic power will not forever elude the world's people. Truth cannot be permanently suppressed. It will rise to the surface of the world's consciousness, free nations and individuals from the tyranny of fear and inspire new decades of achievement.

Around the globe, men and women will acknowledge the wisdom and accept the challenge of words spoken by General George Lee Butler:

> We cannot at once keep sacred the miracle of existence and hold sacrosanct the capacity to destroy it. It is time to reassert the primacy of individual conscience, the voice of reason and the rightful interests of humanity.

Our generation has been on a rising tide. We have the ability to instantly communicate with others around the corner and around the globe. We no longer have to rely on traditional sources of information. The elites who through the years have told us what they wanted us to hear and little more, have lost their ability to control the flow of truth. With the passing of each day, more and more people are gaining the knowledge that will enable them to take charge of their lives and to control the destiny of the nation in which they live.

A World Safe for our Highest Aspirations

In the future, democracy will flourish and so will reverence for human life. People will be better prepared and more willing to accept their responsibilities to themselves, their families and their neighbors. They will better understand the limitations of their leaders and they will not rest until they have made the world safe for our highest aspirations.

The future will not be perfect. But there is every reason to believe that we have been given an opportunity to make it far better than the present or the past. It is an opportunity we must seize or, as Shakespeare put it, ". . . lose our ventures."

Let us join in praying that we will be granted the wisdom to seek and spread the truth and the courage to establish a civilized system of defense. Let us ask for the strength to lift the darkness of fear from human hearts and shine the light of God's healing power on all people, now and forever.

Afterword

Since finishing this book I've come face to face with the threats posed by our government's ill-advised and dangerous military policies. I've become particularly concerned about current plans for an unnecessary and highly questionable missile defense system. The government has spent more than sixty billion dollars on missile defense in the last fifteen years with no functioning system yet to show for it. If Washington presses ahead with this program it will further alienate Russia and China. There are already signs that as a result of the program we may face a renewed nuclear arms competition and once again experience the heightened possibility of nuclear annihilation.

In this and other ways our government has become too arrogant and self-important. We've become so obsessed with defense and being the world's greatest military superpower that we've actually become a threat to ourselves. In everyday language, we've gotten a big head and forgotten that pride goeth before destruction.

If we wish to persuade other nations to become more civilized, we must first come to grips with our own militaristic tendencies. We must take the plank out of our own eye before removing the speck from our brother's eye. We must be prepared to accept for ourselves the standards that we apply to others. If we want and expect other nations to forego the instruments of mass destruction, we must eliminate our own weapons as well. We must strive to see ourselves as others see us. We must recognize the limits of military force and the natural balances that inevitably arise to check the accumulation of excessive power.

I lived through most of the last century—the bloodiest in history. I now witness the beginning of a new millennium and fear that the road we are traveling leads to more war and senseless destruction of life. What have we learned from the past? An excessive reliance on armed force and violence does not work. The only way the United States can retain its present position is through action that is morally and legally consistent. As the world's leading democracy we have a special responsibility to act as a role model for other democratic nations. We must realize that our strength lies in our democratic ideals and economic power, and be willing to trade some of our transitory military might for the more enduring power of trade and cooperation. We must find our liberty in the force of law, not in the law of force.

Index

ABM. *See* Anti-Ballistic Missile Treaty
accidents, catastrophic, 21, 65–67,
   93, 138, 173
Afghanistan, 12, 13, 95, 112–13, 170
Africa, 23, 24, 40
  genocide in, 23, 53, 75
  threats to world order in, 147–48
  See also specific countries
aggression, 92
  anti-, and international
    cooperation, 25, 109, 136
  anti-, and international law, 24,
    26, 84–86, 88, 91–92, 127,
    137, 157
  genocide as form of, 75–76
  Iraq and Saddam Hussein, 3, 12,
    23
  security and, 4, 7
  terrorism and, 70, 74–75
  See also wars
agreements, international, 111
  Dayton agreement as, 44,
    115–16
  foot-dragging on, 50–51, 64, 93
  on-site inspections and, 63, 64,
    136

unenforceable, 22, 25
  See also conventions; ratification;
    treaties
agricultural products, 40–41, 113
Angola, 110, 130
annihilation. *See* catastrophes
Anti-Ballistic Missile Treaty, 163–64
Argentina, 64, 95
armaments, reduction of. *See* arms
  reduction
armed forces. *See* military power
arms control
  CTR program as, 110–11
  nuclear escrow as, 97
  tracking technology for, 9, 10,
    72, 135–36, 138
arms race, 15, 61–62, 77
arms reduction, 1, 35
  for biological and chemical
    weapons, 64–65
  cooperation for, 22, 54–55, 155
  Geneva Disarmament
    Conference and trust in,
    134–35
  for nuclear weapons, 3, 10,
    19–21, 63